DK TRAVEL GUIDES

TURKISH
PHRASE BOOK

A Dorling Kindersley Book

Dorling  Kindersley

LONDON, NEW YORK, SYDNEY, DELHI, PARIS,
MUNICH and JOHANNESBURG

www.dk.com

Compiled by Lexus Ltd with
Ahmet T Türkistanlı and Felicity J Ünlü
Printed and bound in Italy by Printer Trento Srl.

First published in Great Britain in 1998
by Dorling Kindersley Limited
9 Henrietta Street, London WC2E 8PS

Reprinted with corrections 2000
2 4 6 8 10 9 7 5 3 1

Dorling Kindersley books can be purchased in bulk quantities at
discounted prices for use in promotions or as premiums. We are
also able to offer special editions and personalized jackets, corporate
imprints, and excerpts from all of our books, tailored specifically to
meet your own needs. To find out more, please contact: Special Sales,
Dorling Kindersley Limited, 9 Henrietta Street, Covent Garden,
London WC2E 8PS; Tel. 020 7753 3572.

A CIP catalogue record is available from the British Library.

ISBN 0 7513 1089 1

Picture Credits

Jacket: all images special photography DK Studio, Tony Souter,
Clive Streeter and Francesca Yorke.

CONTENTS

Preface   5

Introduction, Pronunciation   6

Useful Everyday Phrases   7

Days, Months, Seasons   13

Numbers   14

Time   15

Hotels   17

Camping and Caravanning   23

Driving   26

Rail and Coach Travel   34

Air Travel   41

By Bus, Taxi and Boat   45

Eating Out   50

Menu Guide   54

Shopping   68

At the Hairdresser   75

Sport   78

Post Offices and Banks   82

Communications   87

Health   93

Conversion Tables   101

Mini-dictionary   104

CONTENTS

PREFACE

This *Dorling Kindersley Travel Guides Phrase Book* has been compiled by experts to meet the general needs of tourists and business travellers. Arranged under headings such as Hotels, Driving and so forth, the ample selection of useful words and phrases is supported by a 2,000-line mini-dictionary. There is also an extensive menu guide listing approximately 550 dishes or methods of cooking and presentation.

Typical replies to questions you may ask during your journey, and the signs or instructions you may see or hear, are shown in tinted boxes. In the main text, the pronunciation of Turkish words and phrases is imitated in English sound syllables. The Introduction gives basic guidelines to Turkish pronunciation.

Dorling Kindersley Travel Guides are recognized as the world's best travel guides. Each title features specially commissioned colour photographs, cutaways of major buildings, 3-D aerial views and detailed maps, plus information on sights, events, hotels, restaurants, shopping and entertainment.

Dorling Kindersley Travel Guides titles include:
Istanbul · Amsterdam · Australia · Sydney
Berlin · Budapest · California · Florida · Hawaii · New York
San Francisco & Northern California · Canada · France · Loire Valley
Paris · Provence · Great Britain · London · Ireland · Dublin
Scotland · Greece: Athens & the Mainland · The Greek Islands · Italy
Florence & Tuscany · Milan & the Lakes · Naples · Rome · Sardinia
Sicily · Venice & the Veneto · Jerusalem & the Holy Land · Mexico
Moscow · St. Petersburg · Portugal · Lisbon · Prague
South Africa · Spain · Barcelona · Madrid · Seville & Andalusia
Thailand · Vienna · Warsaw

INTRODUCTION

Pronunciation

When reading the imitated pronunciation, stress the part that is underlined. Pronounce each syllable as if it formed part of an English word, and you will be understood sufficiently well. Remember the points below, and your pronunciation will be even closer to the correct Turkish.

ay   represents the Turkish **ey** sound and is pronounced as in 'day'.
eh   is pronounced like the 'e' in 'led'.
'eye'   represents the Turkish **ay** sound and is pronounced like the English word 'eye'.
ew   represents the Turkish **ü** sound. This is like the French 'u' or the German 'ü'; pronounce it like the sound in 'few' or 'pew'.
s   is always pronounced as in 'pass', *never* as in 'easy'.
uh   represents the Turkish **ı** sound and is pronounced like the 'i' in 'sir' or the 'er' sound in 'mother'.
ur   represents the Turkish **ö** sound and corresponds to the German 'ö' which is like the 'ur' sound in 'further'.

Summary of Special Turkish Characters

c   (without the cedilla underneath) like 'j' in 'jolly'.
ç   (with cedilla) 'ch' as in 'church'.
ğ   (with breve) is not a 'g' sound at all; it lengthens the preceding vowel.
ı   (looks like an undotted 'i') sounds *uh* – see above.
İ   is a dotted capital 'i'.
ö   (with diaeresis above) sounds *ur* – see above.
ş   (with cedilla) 'sh' as in 'ship'.
ü   (with diaeresis) as in 'few' – see above.

USEFUL EVERYDAY PHRASES

Yes/No
Evet/Hayır
evet/h-'eye'-uhr

Thank you
Teşekkür ederim
teshek-kewr edereem

No, thank you
Hayır, teşekkür ederim
h-'eye'-uhr, teshek-kewr edereem

Please
Lütfen
lewtfen

I don't understand
Anlamıyorum
anlamuhyoroom

Do you speak English/French/German?
İngilizce/Fransızca/Almanca biliyor musunuz?
eengheeleez-jeh/franssuhz-ja/alman-ja beeleyor moo-soonooz

I can't speak Turkish
Türkçe bilmiyorum
tewrk-cheh beelmeeyoroom

Please speak more slowly
Lütfen daha yavaş konuşur musunuz?
lewtfen daha yavash konooshoor moo-soonooz

Please write it down for me
Lütfen yazar mısınız
lewtfen yazar muh-suh-nuhz

Good morning
Günaydın
ghewn-'eye'-duhn

Good afternoon
İyi günler
eeyee ghewn-ler

Good evening
İyi akşamlar
eeyee akshamlar

Good night
İyi geceler
eeyee gheh-jeler

Hello
Merhaba
merhaba

Goodbye
Hoşça kalın
hosh-cha kaluhn

How are you?
Nasılsınız?
nassuhl-suhnuhz

Excuse me, please
Affedersiniz
af-federsseeneez

Sorry!
Özür dilerim!
urzewr deelereem

I'm really sorry
Çok affedersiniz
chok af federsseeneez

Can you help me?
Bana yardım edebilir misiniz?
hana yarduhm edebeeleer mee-seeneez

Can you tell me ...?
... söyleyebilir misiniz?
... surleh-yebeeleer mee-seeneez

Can I have ...?
... rica ediyorum
... reeja edeeyoroom

I would like ...
... istiyorum
... eesteeyoroom

Is there a ... here?
Burada ... var mı?
boorada ... var muh

Where can I get ...?
... nerede bulabilirim?
... neh-reh-deh boolabeeleereem

How much is it?
Bunun fiyatı ne kadar?
boonoon fee-yatuh neh kadar

What time is it?
Saat kaç?
Sa-at kach

I must go now
Şimdi gitmem lazım
sheemdee gheetmem la-zuhm

Cheers!
Şerefe!
sherefeh

Do you take credit cards?
Kredi kartı kabul ediyor musunuz?
kredee kartuh kabool edeeyor moo-soonooz

Can I pay by cheque?
Çekle ödeyebilir miyim?
chekleh urdeh-yebeeleer mee-yeem

Where are the toilets?
Tuvaletler nerede?
toovaletler neh-reh-deh

Are there facilities for the disabled?
Özürlüler için özel olanaklar var mı?
urzewrlewler eecheen urzel olanaklar var muh

Go away!
Çekil!
chekeel

Excellent!
Çok güzel!
chok ghewzel

THINGS YOU'LL SEE OR HEAR

açık	open
afiyet olsun!	enjoy your meal
allahaısmarladık	goodbye (said by person leaving)
arkada	at the back
aşağıda	at the bottom, downstairs
ayrılmış	reserved
basamağa dikkat	mind the step
bayanlar	women
baylar	men
bedava	free
bozuk	out of order
buyurun	please (meaning 'come in', 'sit down', 'go ahead' etc)
cadde	street
çalınız	ring
çalışma saatleri	opening hours
çekiniz	pull
çıkış	way out
çocuklar	children
...-den	from ...
dikkat	attention
dikkat ediniz	take care
döviz	foreign exchange
dur	stop
efendim	sir/madam
efendim?	I beg your pardon?
erkekler	men
fiyat	price
giriniz	enter
giriş	way in, entry
güle güle	goodbye (said by person remaining behind)
gümrük	customs

hızlı	fast
hoş geldiniz!	welcome! (you reply: **hoş bulduk** meaning 'a welcome found')
inşallah!	God willing!
itiniz	push
kadar	until
kadınlar	women
kalkış	departure
kapalı	closed
kasa	till, cash desk
kasaba	town
kiralamak	to rent/hire
kiralık	for rent
kontrol	check, inspection
lütfen	please
maşallah!	wonderful!
memnun oldum	pleased to meet you
meşgul	engaged
ödeyiniz	pay
önde	at the front
sağ	right
satılık	for sale
serbest	free
sigara içilmez	no smoking
sokak	street
sol	left
tarife	charges, price list, timetable
tehlike	danger
varış	arrival
vurunuz	knock
... yasaktır	... not allowed
yavaş	slow
yayalar	pedestrians
yetişkinler	adults
yok	there is none
yukarıda	at the top, above, upstairs

DAYS, MONTHS, SEASONS

Sunday	pazar	*pazar*
Monday	pazartesi	*pazartessee*
Tuesday	salı	*saluh*
Wednesday	çarşamba	*charshamba*
Thursday	perşembe	*pershembeh*
Friday	cuma	*jooma*
Saturday	cumartesi	*joomartessee*
January	ocak	*o-jak*
February	şubat	*shubat*
March	mart	*mart*
April	nisan	*neessan*
May	mayıs	*m-'eye'-uhss*
June	haziran	*hazeeran*
July	temmuz	*tem-mooz*
August	ağustos	*a-oostoss*
September	eylül	*ay-lewl*
October	ekim	*ekeem*
November	kasım	*kassuhm*
December	aralık	*araluhk*
Spring	ilkbahar	*eelk-bahar*
Summer	yaz	*yaz*
Autumn	sonbahar	*sonbahar*
Winter	kış	*kuhsh*
Christmas	Noel	*no-el*
Christmas Eve	Noel Gecesi	*no-el ghejessee*
Easter	Paskalya	*passkalya*
New Year	Yılbaşı	*yuhl-bashuh*
New Year's Eve	Yılbaşı Gecesi	*yuhl-bashuh ghejessee*

13

NUMBERS

0 sıfır *suhfuhr*
1 bir *beer*
2 iki *eekee*
3 üç *ewch*
4 dört *durt*

5 beş *besh*
6 altı *altuh*
7 yedi *yedee*
8 sekiz *sekeez*
9 dokuz *dokooz*

10 on *on*
11 on bir *on beer*
12 on iki *on eekee*
13 on üç *on ewch*
14 on dört *on durt*
15 on beş *on besh*
16 on altı *on altuh*
17 on yedi *on yedee*
18 on sekiz *on sekeez*
19 on dokuz *on dokooz*
20 yirmi *yeermee*
21 yirmi bir *yeermee beer*
22 yirmi iki *yeermee eekee*
23 yirmi üç *yeermee ewch*
30 otuz *otooz*
31 otuz bir *otooz beer*
40 kırk *kuhrk*
50 elli *el-lee*
60 altmış *altmuhsh*
70 yetmiş *yetmeesh*
80 seksen *sekssen*
90 doksan *dokssan*
100 yüz *yewz*
110 yüz on *yewz on*
200 iki yüz *eekee yewz*
1,000 bin *been*
1,000,000 bir milyon *beer meel-yon*
1,000,000,000 bir milyar *beer meel-yar*

14

TIME

today	bugün	booghewn
yesterday	dün	dewn
tomorrow	yarın	yaruhn
the day before	evvelki gün	ev-velkee ghewn
the day after	öbür gün	urbewr ghewn
this week	bu hafta	boo hafta
last week	geçen hafta	ghechen hafta
next week	gelecek hafta	ghelejek hafta
this morning	bu sabah	boo sabah
this afternoon	bugün öğleden sonra	booghewn urleden sonra
this evening	bu akşam	boo aksham
tonight	bu gece	boo ghejeh
yesterday afternoon	dün öğleden sonra	dewn ur leden sonra
last night	dun gece	dewn ghejeh
tomorrow morning	yarın sabah	yaruhn sabah
tomorrow night	yarın gece	yaruhn ghejeh
in three days	uç gün sonra	ewch ghewn sonra
three days ago	üç gün önce	ewch ghewn urn-jeh
late	geç	ghech
early	erken	erken
soon	yakında	yakuhnda
later on	daha sonra	daha sonra
at the moment	şu anda	shoo anda
second	saniye	sanee-yeh
minute	dakika	dakeeka
ten minutes	on dakika	on dakeeka
quarter of an hour	çeyrek saat	chay-rek sa-at
three quarters of an hour	kırk beş dakika	kuhrk besh dakeeka
hour	saat	sa-at
day	gün	ghewn
week	hafta	hafta

fortnight	on beş gün	*on besh ghewn*
month	ay	*'eye'*
year	yıl	*yuhl*

TELLING THE TIME

The simplest way of telling the time in Turkish is by placing the minutes after the hour, eg 'six-fifteen' = **altı on beş**; 'nine-forty' = **dokuz kırk**. Alternatively, the same word order can be used with the addition of **var** (to express 'to') or **geçiyor** (to express 'past'): 'twenty to five' = **beşe yirmi var**; 'ten past eight' = **sekizi on geçiyor. Buçuk** is used for half hours, as in 'three-thirty' – **üç buçuk**; the only exception being 'twelve-thirty' when **yarım** (literally, 'half') is used. The 24-hour clock is widely used, both in timetables and in writing, as well as verbally. There are no equivalents in Turkish to 'am' or 'pm'.

one o'clock	saat bir	*sa-at beer*
ten past one	biri on geçiyor	*beeree on ghecheeyor*
quarter past one	biri çeyrek geçiyor	*beeree chay-rek ghecheeyor*
twenty past one	biri yirmi geçiyor	*beeree yeermee ghecheeyor*
half past one	bir buçuk	*beer boochook*
twenty to two	ikiye yirmi var	*eekee-yeh yeermee var*
quarter to two	ikiye çeyrek var	*eekee-yeh chay-rek var*
ten to two	ikiye on var	*eekee-yeh on var*
two o'clock	saat iki	*sa-at eekee*
13.00	saat on üç	*sa-at on ewch*
16.30	on altı otuz	*on altuh otooz*
20.10	yirmi on	*yeermee on*
at half past five	beş buçukta	*besh boochookta*
at seven o'clock	saat yedide	*sa-at yedeedeh*
noon	öğle	*urleh*
midnight	gece yarısı	*ghejeh yaruhssuh*

HOTELS

Turkish hotels follow the usual five-star classification ranging
from **Lüks** (5-star) to fourth class (1-star). Some hotels are
certified by the government as 'tourist' hotels and such
establishments are obliged to observe certain standards. Many
others are monitored by local authorities. In addition to hotels,
there are also motels, holiday villages, or **tatil köyü** (*tateel
kur-yew*), self-catering apartments, and rooms in private houses,
pansiyon. It's a good idea to have a look at the room before
you take it and to check if the toilet and washbasin are in
working order. Information about hotel accommodation may
be obtained from Tourism and Information offices.

USEFUL WORDS AND PHRASES

balcony	balkon	*balkon*
bathroom	banyo	*ban-yo*
bed	yatak	*yatak*
bedroom	yatak odası	*yatak odassuh*
bill	hesap	*hessap*
blanket	battaniye	*bat-tanee-yeh*
breakfast	kahvaltı	*kahvaltuh*
cold water	soğuk su	*so-ook soo*
cot	çocuk yatağı	*chojook yata-uh*
dining room	yemek salonu	*yemek salonoo*
dinner	akşam yemeği	*aksham yemehee*
double room	iki kişilik oda	*eekee keesheeleek oda*
foyer	giriş holü,	*gheereesh holew,*
	fuaye	*fw-'eye'-yeh*
full board	tam pansiyon	*tam pansseeyon*
half board	yarım pansiyon	*yaruhm pansseeyon*
hotel	otel	*otel*
hot water	sıcak su	*suhjak soo*
key	anahtar	*anahtar*
lift	asansör	*assanssur*
lounge	salon	*salon*

lunch	öğle yemeği	*ur-leh yemeh-ee*
manager	müdür	*mewdewr*
plug	tıkaç	*tuhkach*
receipt	makbuz	*makbooz*
reception	resepsiyon	*ressepsseeyon*
receptionist	resepsiyon görevlisi	*ressepsseeyon gurevleessee*
restaurant	lokanta, restoran	*lokanta, restoran*
room	oda	*oda*
room service	oda servisi	*oda serveessee*
shower	duş	*doosh*
single room	tek kişilik oda	*tek keesheeleek oda*
toilet	tuvalet	*toovalet*
toilet paper	tuvalet kağıdı	*toovalet ka-uh duh*
twin room	çift yataklı oda	*cheeft yatakluh oda*
washbasin	lavabo	*lavabo*

Have you any vacancies?
Boş odanız var mı?
bosh odanuhz var muh

I have a reservation
Rezervasyonum var
rezervass-yonoom var

I'd like a single room
Tek kişilik bir oda istiyorum
tek keesheeleek beer oda eesteeyoroom

We'd like a double room
İki kişilik bir oda istiyoruz
eekee kesheeleek beer oda eesteeyorooz

Do you have a twin room?
Çift yataklı bir odanız var mı?
cheeft yatakluh beer odanuhz var muh

I'd like a room with a bathroom/balcony
Banyolu/balkonlu bir oda istiyorum
ban-yoloo/balkonloo beer odạ eesteeyọroom

Is there satellite/cable TV in the rooms?
Odalarda uydu televizyonu/kablolu televizyon var mı?
odalarda ooydoo tele-veezyonoo/kabloloo tele-veezyon var muh

I'd like a room for one night/three nights
Bir/üç gece için bir oda istiyorum
beer/ewch ghejẹh eechẹen beer odạ eesteeyọroom

I don't know yet how long I'll stay
Ne kadar kalacağımı henüz bilmiyorum
neh kadạr kalaja-uhmuh henẹwz bẹelmeeyoroom

What is the charge per night?
Bir gecelik ücreti ne kadar?
beer ghejeleek ewjretee neh kadạr

May I have a look at the room?
Odayı görebilir miyim?
od-'eye'-yụh gurebeelẹer meeyẹem

When is breakfast/dinner?
Kahvaltı/akşam yemeği saat kaçta?
kahvaltụh/akshạm yemẹh-ee sạ-at kạchta

Would you have my luggage brought up?
Lütfen bavullarımı odama çıkartın
lẹwtfen bavoolaruhmụh odamạ chuhkartụhn

Please call me at … o'clock
Lütfen beni saat …-da uyandırın
lẹwtfen benẹe sạ-at …-da oo-yanduhrụhn

Can I have breakfast in my room?
Odamda kahvaltı edebilir miyim?
odamda kahvaltuh edebeeleer meeyeem

I'll be back at ... o'clock
Saat ...-de döneceğim
sa-at ...-deh durnejeh-eem

My room number is ...
... numarada kalıyorum
... noomarada kaluhyoroom

I'm leaving tomorrow
Yarın ayrılıyorum
yaruhn 'eye'-ruhluhyoroom

May I have my bill, please?
Hesabımı rica ediyorum
hessabuhmuh reeja edeeyoroom

Can you recommend another hotel?
Başka bir otel tavsiye edebilir misiniz?
bashka beer otel tavssee-yeh edebeeleer mee-seeneez

Can you get me a taxi?
Lüften bana bir taksi çağırır mısınız?
lewtfen bana beer takssee cha-uhruhr muh-suh-nuhz

I've lost my room key
Oda anahtarımı kaybettim
oda anahtaruhmuh k-'eye'-betteem

The toilet won't flush
Tuvalet tıkandı
toovalet tuhkanduh

There's no water
Su yok
soo yok

There's no plug in the washbasin
Lavaboda tıkaç yok
lavaboda tuhkach yok

THINGS YOU'LL SEE

akşam yemeği	dinner
asansör	lift
bagaj	luggage
balkon	balcony
banyo	bath
basın	press
çekin	pull
çift yataklı oda	twin room
çocuklar	children
dolu	full, no vacancies
duş	shower
gece	night
hesap	bill
iki kişilik oda	double room
kahvaltı	breakfast
kahvaltı dahil	breakfast included
kat	floor, storey
KDV	VAT
komple kahvaltı	full breakfast
oda	room
öğle yemeği	lunch
pansiyon	bed in a private house (not always with breakfast)
resepsiyon	reception
rezervasyon	reservation

⟶

şofben	water heater
tam pansiyon	full board
tek kişilik oda	single room
tuvalet	toilet
yangın çıkışı	emergency exit
yarım pansiyon	half board
yemek salonu	dining room
zemin kat	ground floor

THINGS YOU'LL HEAR

Hiç iki kişilik odamız kalmadı
We have no double rooms left

Maalesef doluyuz
I'm sorry, we're full

Kaç gecelik?
For how many nights?

Lütfen odayı …-de boşaltın
Please vacate the room by…

Lütfen ücreti peşin ödeyin
Please pay in advance

CAMPING AND CARAVANNING

In Turkey there are still not very many well-equipped, 'approved' campsites but adequate campsites, sometimes with private beaches, may be found on principal routes and at tourist centres. Campsites are generally open from April or May until October. Camping on private ground away from official campsites requires the landlord's permission. Some student hostels double as youth hostels during vacations.

USEFUL WORDS AND PHRASES

bucket	kova	kova
campfire	kamp ateşi	kamp ateshee
to go camping	kamp yapmak	kamp yapmak
campsite	kamp yeri	kamp yeree
caravan	karavan	karavan
caravan site	kamping	kampeeng
cooking utensils	kap kacak	kap kajak
drinking water	içme suyu	eechmeh soo-yoo
ground sheet	su geçirmez yaygı	soo ghech-eer-mez yay-guh
guy rope	çadır ipi	chaduhr eepee
to hitchhike	otostop yapmak	otostop yapmak
rope	ip	eep
rubbish	çöp	churp
rucksack	sırt çantası	suhrt chantassuh
saucepans	tencereler	tenjereh-ler
sleeping bag	uyku tulumu	ooy-koo tooloomoo
tent	çadır	chaduhr
youth hostel	gençlik yurdu	ghench-leek yurdoo

Can I camp here?
Burada kamp yapabilir miyim?
boorada kamp yapabeeleer mee-yeem

Can we park the caravan here?
Karavanı buraya park edebilir miyiz?
karavanuh boora-ya park edebeeleer mee-yeez

Where is the nearest campsite/caravan site?
En yakın kamp yeri/kamping nerede?
en yakuhn kamp yeree/kampeeng neh-reh-deh

What is the charge per night?
Bir gecelik ücreti kaç lira?
beer gheh-jeh-leek ewj-retee kach leera

What facilities are there?
Ne gibi imkanlar var?
neh gheebee eemkanlar var

Can I light a fire here?
Burada ateş yakabilir miyim?
boorada atesh yakabeeleer mee-yeem

Where can I get …?
Nerede … bulabilirim?
neh-reh-deh … boolabeeleereem

Is there drinking water here?
Burada içme suyu var mı?
boorada eechmeh soo-yoo var muh

THINGS YOU'LL SEE OR HEAR

ateş	fire
battaniye	blanket
çadır	tent
çadır bezi	tarpaulin
çadır direği	tent pole
çadır kazığı	tent peg
duş	shower
ışık	light
içme suyu	drinking water
kamp ateşi	campfire
kamp yapmak yasaktır	no camping
kamp yeri	campsite
karavan	caravan
kimlik	identification
kira ücreti	hire charge
kullanım	use
mutfak	kitchen
römorkör	trailer
tuvalet	toilet
uyku tulumu	sleeping bag
ücretler	charges
yasak	not permitted
yasak bölge	restricted zone
yatakhane	dormitory

DRIVING

The national highway network mostly consists of single-lane asphalt roads which connect all major cities and towns. These inter-city links are able to cope with the relatively low volume of traffic. A motorway, **otoyol** (*otoyol*), for which a toll is charged, links Istanbul to Ankara. There are also short stretches of motorway around Istanbul, Izmir, Izmit, and at both ends of the Bosphorus Bridge – **çevre yolu** (*chevre yoloo*) – which are free of charge. Secondary roads are fairly poor in quality and are mostly surfaced with gravel chippings.

The Turkish traffic code is similar to that in European countries, the rule being that you drive on the right and overtake on the left. International traffic signs are used. Traffic coming from the right has priority at crossroads and junctions wherever there are no priority signs or traffic lights.

In built-up areas a speed limit of 50 km/h (31 mph) is shown by a red-bordered circular sign with the number 50 in black. A similar black and white sign with black diagonal stripes signals the end of the speed limit. Outside built-up areas, the general speed limit is 90 km/h (56 mph) and 80 km/h (50 mph) for lorries and vans. All roads in Turkey are made hazardous by reckless driving and extreme caution is recommended.

Drivers entering Turkey by car from abroad should have a green card certificate of insurance. Your passport will be endorsed upon entry and this must be cancelled before you can leave the country. Turkey's comprehensive intercity coach network means that a car is not necessary for travelling to other cities but, if you do wish to hire a car while there, you will find both international and Turkish hire companies in Istanbul and Ankara. An international licence is not required.

There are plenty of petrol stations on main roads, and most of them stay open 24 hours. Many have restaurants and shops attached to them.

SOME COMMON ROAD SIGNS

azami genişlik	maximum width
azami hız	maximum speed
azami park 1 saat	parking limited to 1 hour
azami yükseklik	maximum height
çıkış	exit
çıkmaz sokak	cul-de-sac
daralan kaplama	road narrows
devamlı virajlar	series of bends
dikkat	caution
döner kavşak	roundabout
dur	stop
durmak yasaktır	no stopping
durulmaz	no stopping
ekspres yolun sonu	end of motorway
geç	cross
geçme yasağı	no overtaking
geri dönülmez	no U-turns
gevşek malzeme	loose chippings
gevşek şev	falling rock
hemzemin geçit	level crossing
hız kısıtlaması sonu	end of speed restriction
iki yönlü trafik	two-way traffic
karşıdan gelen taşıtlara öncelik	oncoming traffic has right of way
kasis	uneven road surface
kavşak	junction
kaygan yol	slippery road
otopark	car park
park yapılmaz	no parking
sağa dönülmez	no right turn
sağa/sola viraj	bend to right/left
sağdan gidiniz	keep to the right
sert viraj	sharp bend
sola dönülmez	no left turn

→

tali yol kavşağı	crossroads
taşıt giremez	no entry for vehicles
taşıt trafiğine kapalı yol	closed to all vehicles
tehlikeli eğim	steep gradient
tek yönlü yol	one-way street
tren yolu geçidi	level crossing
viraj	bend
yavaş	drive slowly
yaya geçidi	pedestrian crossing
yol kapalı	road closed
yol ver	give way
yolda çalışma	roadworks

USEFUL WORDS AND PHRASES

automatic	otomatik	*otomateek*
boot	bagaj	*bagaj*
brake	fren	*fren*
breakdown	arıza	*aruhza*
car	otomobil, araba	*otomobeel, araba*
caravan	karavan	*karavan*
clutch	debriyaj	*debreeyaj*
crossroads	tali yol kavşağı	*talee yol kavsha-uh*
to drive	sürmek	*sewrmek*
engine	motor	*motor*
exhaust	egzoz	*egzos*
fanbelt	vantilatör kayışı	*vanteelatur k-'eye'-yuhshuh*
garage	garaj	*garaj*
gear	vites	*veetess*
gears	vitesler	*veetessler*
gearbox	vites kutusu	*veetess kootoossoo*
junction *(motorway)*	kavşak	*kavshak*
licence	ehliyet	*ehleeyet*

lights (*head*)	farlar	*farlar*
(*rear*)	arka lambalar	*arka lambalar*
lorry	kamyon	*kam-yon*
manual	düz	*dewz*
mirror	ayna	*'eye'-na*
motorbike	motosiklet	*motoseeklet*
motorway	ekspresyol	*ekspress-yol*
number plate	plaka	*plaka*
petrol	benzin	*benzeen*
petrol station	benzin istasyonu	*benzeen eestass-yonoo*
road	yol	*yol*
skid	kayma	*k-'eye'-ma*
spares	yedek parçalar	*yedek parchalar*
speed	hız	*huhz*
speed limit	hız tahdidi	*huhz tahdeedee*
speedometer	kilometre saati	*keelometreh sa-atee*
steering wheel	direksiyon	*deereksseeyon*
to tow (*away*)	çekmek	*chekmek*
traffic lights	trafik ışıkları	*trafeek uhshuhk-laruh*
trailer	römork	*rurmork*
tyre	dışlastik	*duhsh-lasteek*
van	kamyonet	*kam-yonet*
wheel	tekerlek	*tekerlek*
windscreen	ön cam	*urn jam*
windscreen	silecek	*seelejek*
wiper		

I need some petrol
Biraz benzine ihtiyacım var
beeraz benzeeneh eehtee-yajuhm var

I need some oil
Biraz yağa ihtiyacım var
beeraz ya-a eehtee-yajuhm var

29

Fill it up, please!
Lütfen depoyu doldurun!
lewtfen depo-yoo doldooroon

I'd like 10 litres of petrol
Lütfen 10 litre benzin
lewtfen on leetreh benzeen

Would you check the tyres, please?
Lütfen lastikleri kontrol eder misiniz?
lewtfen lasteekleree kontrol eder mee-seeneez

Where is the nearest garage?
En yakın garaj nerede?
en yakuhn garaj neh-reh-deh

How do I get to …?
…-e nasıl gidebilirim?
…-eh nasuhl gheedebeeleereem

Is this the road to …?
… yolu bu mu?
… yoloo boo moo

Where can I park?
Nereye park edebilirim?
neh-reh-yeh park edebeeleereem

Can I park here?
Buraya park edebilir miyim?
boora-ya park edebeeleer mee-yeem

I'd like to hire a car
Bir otomobil kiralamak istiyorum
beer otomobeel keeralamak eesteeyoroom

Can we hire a baby/child (car) seat?
bebek/çocuk koltuğu kiralayabilir miyiz?
behbek/chojook koltoo-oo keera-layabeleer meeyeez

Is there a mileage charge?
Ayrıca kilometre ücreti var mı?
'eye'-ruhja keelometreh ewjretee var muh

Do you do repairs?
Tamir işleri yapıyor musunuz?
tameer eeshleree yapuhyor moo-soonooz

Can you repair the clutch?
Debriyajı tamir edebilir misiniz?
debree-yajuh tameer edebeeleer mee-seeneez

How long will it take?
Ne kadar sürer?
neh kadar sewrer

There is something wrong with the engine
Motorda bir arıza var
motorda beer aruhza var

The engine is overheating
Motor fazla ısınıyor
motor fazla uhsuhnuh-yor

The brakes are binding
Pedala basılınca frenler sıkışıyor
pedala basuhluhnja frenler suhkuh-shuhyor

I need a new tyre
Yeni bir lastik lazım
yenee beer lasteek la-zuhm

DIRECTIONS YOU MAY BE GIVEN

çok uzak	it's a long way
çok yakın	it's very near
doğru gidin	go straight on
dümdüz devam edin	straight on
geri gidin	go back
...-i geçin	go past the ...
ikinci yoldan sapın	take the second turning
ilk yoldan sapın	take the first turning
sağ	right
sağa dönün	turn right
sağdan birinci	first on the right
sol	left
sola dönün	turn left
soldan ikinci	second on the left

THINGS YOU'LL HEAR

Otomatik mi düz vitesli mi istersiniz?
Would you like an automatic or a manual?

Ehliyetinizi verin, lütfen
May I see your licence?

THINGS YOU'LL SEE

benzin	petrol, fuel
benzin istasyonu	fuel/petrol station
benzin pompası	petrol pump
cam sileceği	windscreen wiper
çıkış	exit
ekspresyol	motorway
ekspresyol kavşağı	motorway junction
gaz vermek	to accelerate
harita	map
hava basıncı	air pressure
kasis	uneven road surface
kenar şeridi	hard shoulder
kontrol etmek	to check
köy yolu	country road
kurşunsuz	lead-free petrol
lastik basıncı	tyre pressure
mazot	diesel
ön cam	windscreen, windshield
süper	4-star
tali yol kavşağı	crossroads
tamir etmek	to repair
taşıt kuyruğu	tailback
trafik tıkanıklığı	traffic jam
yağ	oil
yağ seviyesi	oil level
yan geçit	bypass
yavaş vasıta şeridi	crawler lane
yedek depo	spare tank

RAIL AND COACH TRAVEL

Turkish State Railways (TCDD) connect most major cities but
are not famous for their efficiency. The best trains to travel by
are the **ekspres** trains, especially those operating between
Izmir, Ankara and Istanbul, which are usually first class only.
Long-distance trains have couchettes, sleeping cars and dining
cars. There are discounts for students and on return tickets.

The extensive coach network covering all Turkish towns and
cities provides a popular, faster and more efficient alternative
to trains. Coaches are cheap and run at frequent intervals, both
day and night. The coaches are very comfortable and usually
contain a mini fridge at the back with bottles of cold drinking
water, **içme suyu** (*eechmeh soo-yoo*), which passengers are free
to help themselves to. It is also the custom for lemon cologne
to be brought round and sprinkled onto passengers' cupped
hands during the journey. On long-distance journeys stops are
made and passengers can buy refreshments both outside and
inside the coach from sellers of various types of food, the most
famous of these being the **simitçi** (*seemeet-chee*), or **simit**
seller. This is usually a small boy balancing on his head a round
tray of **simit** – bread rings covered with sesame seeds.

USEFUL WORDS AND PHRASES

booking office	bilet gişesi	*beelet ghee-shessee*
buffet	büfe	*bewfeh*
carriage	vagon	*vagon*
coach	otobüs	*otobewss*
coach terminal	otogar	*otogar*
communication cord	imdat freni	*eemdat frenee*
compartment	kompartıman	*kompartuhman*
connection	bağlantı	*ba-lantuh*
currency exchange	döviz	*durveez*
dining car	vagon restoran	*vagon restoran*
driver	şoför	*shofur*
engine	lokomotif	*lokomoteef*

34

entrance	giriş	*gheereesh*
exit	çıkış	*chuh-kuhsh*
first class	birinci sınıf	*beereenjee suh-nuhf*
to get in	binmek	*been-mek*
to get out	inmek	*een-mek*
guard	kondüktör	*kondewk-tur*
indicator board	gösterge levhası	*gurster-gheh levhassuh*
left luggage	emanet	*emanet*
lost property	kayıp eşya	*k-'eye'-uhp esh-ya*
luggage locker	emanet kasası	*emanet kassassuh*
luggage rack	bagaj rafı	*bagaj rafuh*
luggage trolley	eşya arabası	*esh-ya arabassuh*
luggage van	bagaj vagonu	*bagaj vagonoo*
platform	peron	*peron*
rail	ray	*r-'eye'*
railway	demiryolu	*demeer-yoloo*
reserved seat	ayrılmış yer	*'eye'-ruhl-muhsh yer*
restaurant car	vagon restoran	*vagon restoran*
return ticket	gidiş dönüş bileti	*gheedeesh durnewsh beeletee*
second class	ikinci sınıf	*eekeenjee suh-nuhf*
single ticket	gidiş bileti	*gheedeesh beeletee*
sleeping car	yataklı vagon	*yatahluh vagon*
station	istasyon	*eestass-yon*
station master	gar şefi	*gar shefee*
ticket	bilet	*beelet*
ticket collector	kondüktör	*kondewk-tur*
timetable	tarife	*tareefeh*
tracks	raylar	*r-'eye'-lar*
train	tren	*tren*
waiting room	bekleme salonu	*beklemeh salonoo*
window	pencere	*penjereh*

When does the train for ... leave?
... treni saat kaçta kalkıyor?
... trenee sa-at kachta kalkuh-yor

When does the train from ... arrive?
... treni saat kaçta gelecek?
... trenee sa-at kachta ghelejek

When is the next train to ...?
...-e bundan sonraki tren saat kaçta?
...-eh boondan sonrakee tren sa-at kachta

When is the first train to ...?
...-e ilk tren saat kaçta?
...-eh eelk tren sa-at kachta

When is the last train to ...?
...-e son tren saat kaçta?
...-eh son tren sa-at kachta

What is the fare to ...?
...-ya bir bilet kaç lira?
...-ya beer beelet kach leera

Do we have to pay for the children?
Çocuklar için para ödememiz gerekiyor mu?
chojooklar eecheen parah urdememeez gherekeeyor moo

Do I have to change?
Aktarma yapmam lazım mı?
aktarma yapmam la-zuhm muh

Does the train stop at ...?
Tren ...-de duruyor mu?
tren ...-deh doorooyor moo

How long does it take to get from ... to ...?
...-den ...-e kadar yol ne kadar sürer?
...-den ...-eh kadar yol neh kadar sewrer

A single/return ticket to …, please
Lütfen, …-e bir gidiş/gidiş dönüş bileti
lewtfen, …-eh beer gheedeesh/gheedeesh durnewsh beeletee

Do I have to pay a supplement?
Fark ödemem gerekiyor mu?
fark urdemem gherekeeyor moo

I'd like to reserve a seat
Bir yer ayırtmak istiyorum
beer yer 'eye'-uhrt-mak eesteeyoroom

Is this the right train for …?
Bu … treni midir?
boo … trenee meedeer

Is this the right platform for the … train?
… treni bu perondan mı kalkıyor?
… trenee boo perondan muh kalkuh-yor

Which platform for the … train?
… treni hangi perondan kalkıyor?
… trenee hanghee perondan kalkuh-yor

Is the train late?
Tren gecikti mi?
tren ghejeektee mee

Could you help me with my luggage, please?
Lütfen eşyalarımı taşımama yardım eder misiniz?
lewtfen esh-yalaruhmuh tashuh-mama yarduhm eder mee-seeneez

Is this a non-smoking compartment?
Bu kompartıman sigara içmeyenlere mi mahsus?
boo kompartuhman seegara eechmayenlereh mee mah-sooss

Is this seat free?
Bu yer boş mu?
boo yer bosh moo

This seat is taken
Bu yerin sahibi var
boo yereen saheebee var

I have reserved this seat
Bu yeri ben ayırttım
boo yeree ben 'eye'-uhrt-tuhm

May I open/close the window?
Pencereyi açabilir/kapatabilir miyim?
penjereh-yee acha-beeleer/kapata-beeleer mee-yeem

When do we arrive in …?
…-e ne zaman varıyoruz?
…-eh neh zaman varuh-yorooz

What station is this?
Bu istasyonun adı nedir?
boo eestass-yonoon aduh nedeer

When does my connection leave?
Aktarma yapacağım tren kaçta kalkıyor?
aktarma yapaja-uhm tren kachta kalkuh-yor

Do we stop at …?
…-de duruyor muyuz?
…-deh doorooyor moo-yooz

Is there a restaurant car on this train?
Bu trende vagon restoran var mı?
boo trendeh vagon restoran var muh?

THINGS YOU'LL HEAR

Tren ...-den kalkmak üzeredir
The train is about to depart from ...

Bir sonraki tren saat ...-dadır
The next train is at ...

Yalnız birinci sınıf bilet var
There are only first-class seats

...-de aktarma yapmanız gerekir
You have to change at ...

Fark ödeyeceksiniz
You must pay a supplement

Tren rötarlı
The train is late

THINGS YOU'LL SEE

aktarma yapınız	change
ayrılmış yer	reserved seat
bekleme salonu	waiting room
bilet farkı	fare supplement
biletler	tickets
bilet otomatı	ticket machine
bininiz	get on board
boş	vacant
büfe	fast-food counter
Cumartesileri	Saturdays
çıkılmaz	no exit
çıkış	exit
danışma	information
...-de durmaz	does not stop at ...
dışarı sarkmayınız	do not lean out

→

dikkat	attention
döviz	currency exchange
ekspres	express
ekspres farkı	express train supplement
emanet	left luggage
emanet kasaları	luggage lockers
gecikme	delay
giriş	entry
... günleri dışında	... days excepted
güzergah	route
imdat freni	emergency cord
inmek	to get off/out
kalkış	departure
kapıları kapatınız	close the doors
kuşet	couchette
merkez istasyonu	central station
meşgul	engaged
otobüs	coach
otogar	coach station
Pazar ve tatil günleri	Sundays and holidays
peron	platform
rötar	delay
seyahat	journey
seyahat hakkında bilgi	travel information
sigara içenler	smokers
sigara içmeyenler	non-smokers
şoför	driver
tarife	timetable
tatil	holidays
tuvalet	toilet
vagon	carriage, car
vagon restoran	restaurant car
varış	arrival
yalnız ... günleri	... days only
yataklı vagon	sleeping car
yer ayırtma	seat reservation

AIR TRAVEL

Turkish Airlines (THY) operate scheduled flights to all major
cities in the country. Flights between Izmir, Ankara and
Istanbul are fairly frequent. There are discounts of around
50 per cent for children and sports groups, and 25 per cent for
students. There are also private airlines which provide
domestic flights between various regions but details of these
are not always available outside Turkey.

USEFUL WORDS AND PHRASES

aircraft	uçak	oochak
air hostess	hostes	hostess
airline	havayolu	hava-yoloo
airport	havalimanı	havaleemanuh
airport bus	havalimanı otobüsü	havaleemanuh otobewssew
aisle	koridor	koreedor
arrival	varış	varuhsh
baggage claim	bagaj alma yeri	bagaj alma yeree
boarding card	biniş kartı	beeneesh kartuh
check-in	bagaj kaydı	bagaj k-'eye'-duh
check-in desk	bagaj kayıt masası	bagaj k-'eye'-uht massassuh
customs	gümrük	ghewmrewk
delay	gecikme	ghejeekmeh
departure	kalkış	kalkuhsh
departure lounge	giden yolcular salonu	gheeden yoljoolar salonoo
emergency exit	imdat çıkışı	eemdat chuh-kuhshuh
flight	uçuş	oochoosh
flight number	uçuş numarası	oochoosh noomarassuh
gate	çıkış kapısı	chuh-kuhsh kapuh-suh
jet	jet	jet
to land	inmek	eenmek
passport	pasaport	passaport

passport control	pasaport kontrolü	*passaport kontrolew*
pilot	pilot	*peelot*
runway	pist	*peest*
seat	koltuk	*koltook*
seat belt	emniyet kemeri	*emneeyet kemeree*
steward	kabin memuru	*kabeen memooroo*
stewardess	hostes	*hostess*
take off	kalkmak	*kalkmak*
window	pencere	*penjereh*
wing	kanat	*kanat*

When is there a flight to ...?
...-ye ne zaman uçak var?
...-yeh neh zaman oochak var

What time does the flight to ... leave?
... uçağı saat kaçta kalkıyor?
... oocha-uh sa-at kachta kalkuh-yor

Is it a direct flight?
Direkt sefer midir?
deerekt sefer meedeer

Do I have to change planes?
Uçak değiştirmem gerekiyor mu?
oochak deh-eeshteermem gherekeeyor moo

When do I have to check in?
Bagajımı ne zaman kaydettirmem gerekiyor?
bagajuhmuh neh zaman k-'eye'-det-teermem gherekeeyor

I'd like a single/return ticket to ...
... bir gidiş/gidiş dönüş bileti istiyorum
... beer gheedeesh/gheedeesh durnewsh beeletee eesteeyoroom

I'd like a non-smoking seat, please
Lütfen, sigara içilmeyen kısımdan bir yer verin
lewtfen, seegara eecheelmayen kuhsuhmdan beer yer vereen

I'd like a smoking seat, please
Lütfen, sigara içilen kısımdan bir yer verin
lewtfen, seegara eecheelen kuhsuhmdan beer yer vereen

I'd like a window seat, please
Lütfen, pencere yanından bir yer verin
lewtfen, penjereh yanuhndan beer yer vereen

How long will the flight be delayed?
Uçak ne kadar gecikecek?
oochak neh kadar ghejeekeh-jek

Is this the right gate for the … flight?
… uçağı için çıkış kapısı bu mudur?
… oocha-uh eecheen chuh-kuhsh kapuh-suh boo moodoor

When do we arrive in …?
…-ye saat kaçta varacağız?
…-yeh sa-at kachta varaja-uhz

May I smoke now?
Şimdi sigara içebilir miyim?
sheemdee seegara eecheh-beeleer mee-yeem

THINGS YOU'LL SEE OR HEAR

ara durak	intermediate stop
bagaj alma yeri	baggage claim
bagaj kaydı	check-in
bagaj kaydını yaptırmak	to check in
bagaj kayıt masası	check-in desk

→

43

bagaj kontrolü	baggage check
çek-in	check-in
çıkış kapısı	gate
danışma	information
direkt sefer	direct flight
el bagajı	hand luggage
emniyet kemerlerinizi bağlayınız	fasten seat belts
enformasyon	information
gecikme	delay
gümrük	customs
hareket	departure
imdat çıkışı	emergency exit
iniş	landing
irtifa	altitude
mecburi iniş	emergency landing
pasaport kontrolü	passport control
sefer	flight
sigara içenler	smokers
sigara içilmez	no smoking
sigara içmeyenler	non-smokers
sigara içmeyiniz	refrain from smoking
tarifeli sefer	scheduled flight
uçak	aircraft
uçuş hızı	flight speed
uçuş süresi	flight time
uçuşa hazır	ready for takeoff
varış	arrival
yerel saat	local time
yolcular	passengers

BY BUS, TAXI AND BOAT

Major Turkish cities and towns have bus networks which, though cheap, are generally crowded. Most work on a ticket system which requires a ticket or a book of tickets to be bought beforehand from a ticket kiosk.

In large cities such as Istanbul, Ankara and Izmir, the overworked bus services are supplemented by a system of shared taxis, called **dolmuş** (*dolmoosh*), often capable of carrying 8–10 passengers. These operate between fixed destinations, but the passenger can get in and out at stops en route and pays according to the distance travelled. **Dolmuşes**, which are usually recognizable by a yellow strip around them, are more expensive than buses but cheaper than taxis. Outside cities they run between small towns and villages.

Taxis are numerous throughout Turkey and are distinguished by their yellow colour. Taxi meters are generally fitted. Taxis may at times operate as **dolmuşes**.

Istanbul and Ankara both have Metro systems, which run above and below ground. Istanbul also has a modern tram network which, together with the Metro, provides a comprehensive transport system.

One of the most pleasant ways of getting around Istanbul is by ferry – **vapur** (*vapoor*). These provide public transport to various locations on both sides of the Bosphorus and the Princes' Islands. The popular tour which zig-zags up the Bosphorus is well worth trying. There are also catamarans known as 'sea buses', **deniz otobüsleri** (*deneez otobewss-leree*), which offer several routes and are faster than the **vapur** but more expensive. Some larger boats provide regular services for travelling to the ports along the Black Sea, the Mamara and to the Aegean and Mediterranean coasts.

In Istanbul, it may make sense to buy an **AKBİL** (*akbeel*, short for **akıllı bilet** or 'intelligent ticket'), a token which can be used on most types of public transport and is rechargeable.

USEFUL WORDS AND PHRASES

adult	yetişkin	yeteesh-keen
boat	vapur	vapoor
book of tickets	küpür bilet	kewpewr beelet
bus	otobüs	otobewss
bus station	otobüs garajı, otogar	otobewss garajuh, otogar
bus stop	otobüs durağı	otobewss doora-uh
child	çocuk	chojook
coach	otobüs	otobewss
conductor	biletçi	beelet-chee
connection	bağlantı	ba-lantuh
cruise	vapur gezisi	vapoor ghezeessee
driver	şoför	shofur
fare	ücret	ewj-ret
ferry	araba vapuru	araba vapooroo
lake	göl	gurl
number 5 bus	5 numaralı otobüs	besh numaraluh otobewss
passenger	yolcu	yoljoo
port	liman	leeman
quay	iskele	eess-keleh
river	nehir	neheer
sea	deniz	deneez
seat	yer	yer
ship	gemi	ghemee
station	istasyon	eestass-yon
taxi	taksi	taksee
terminus	son durak	son doorak
ticket	bilet	beelet

Where is the bus station?
Otogar nerede?
otogar neh-reh-deh

Where is there a bus stop?
Nerede otobüs durağı var?
neh-reh-deh otobewss doora-uh var

Which buses go to …?
Hangi otobüsler …-e gider?
hanghee otobewss-ler …-eh gheedeer

How often do the buses to … run?
…-e giden otobüslerin arası ne kadardır?
…-eh gheeden otobewss-lereen arassuh neh kadar-duhr

Could you tell me when we get to …?
…-e varınca bana haber verir misiniz?
…-eh varuhn-ja bana haber vereer mee-seeneez

Do I have to get off yet?
İneceğim yere geldik mi?
eenejeh-eem yereh gheldeek mee

How do you get to … from here?
Buradan …-e nasıl gidilir?
booradan …-eh nassuhl gheedeeleer

Is it very far?
Çok uzak mı?
chok oozak muh

I want to go to …
…-e gitmek istiyorum
…-eh gheet-mek eesteeyoroom

Do you go near …?
… yakınından geçiyor musunuz?
*… yak*u*hn-uhndan ghecheey*o*r moo-soon*oo*z*

Where can I buy a ticket?
Nereden bilet alabilirim?
*n*e*h-reh-den beel*e*t ala-beel*ee*reem*

Please close/open the window
Lütfen, pencereyi açın/kapayın
*l*e*wtfen, penjereh-y*ee *ach*u*hn/kap-'eye'-y*u*hn*

Could you help me get a ticket?
Bilet almama yardım eder misiniz?
*beel*e*t almam*a *yard*u*hm ed*e*r mee-seen*ee*z*

When does the last bus leave?
Son otobüs saat kaçta kalkıyor?
*son otob*e*wss s*a*-at k*a*chta kalkuh-y*o*r*

THINGS YOU'LL SEE OR HEAR

abone kartı	season ticket
aylık bilet	monthly season ticket
banliyö tren şebekesi	local railway system
bilet	ticket
bozuk para	change (noun: money)
çıkış	exit
değiştirmek	to change (transport)
dolmuş	collective taxi
dolmuş durağı	collective taxi stand
duracak yer	standing room
durak	stop
gidiş dönüş bileti	return ticket
girilmez	no entry

→

giriş	entry
gösteriniz	show
günlük bilet	day ticket
haftalık bilet	weekly ticket
imdat çıkışı	emergency exit
imdat freni	emergency brake
iskele	boarding/landing pier
istasyon	station
kalkış	departure
kısa yolculuk	short journey
kontrolör	inspector
minibüs	minibus
otobüs garajı, otogar	bus station
otobüs/tren bileti	bus/train ticket
oturaçak yer	seat
ödeyiniz	pay
öğrenci kartı	student pass
önden/arkadan binilir	entry at front/back
özürlü kişiler	disabled people
ray	track
sigara içmek yasaktır	no smoking
son durak	terminus
şoför	driver
tam ücret	exact fare
Tünel	original Istanbul underground
vapur	passenger ferry
varış	arrival
yalnız gidiş	single journey
yetişkinler	adults

EATING OUT

There is a good choice of restaurants – **lokanta** – for the tourist who wishes to sample Turkish food. These range from expensive establishments to humble eating places offering a limited number of dishes. Not all restaurants will have a menu. If there is no menu the restaurant will rely on the waiter to tell the customers what is available or to invite them through to the kitchen to have a look at the dishes. There are also restaurants which specialize in certain types of food:

Kebapçı (*kebap-chuh*): these are meat restaurants which the vegetarian would be well advised to avoid. The meat, mostly lamb, is grilled or barbecued in various ways and eaten with salads. They feature regional varieties such as **Urfa Kebabı** (*oorfa kebabuh*) – very hot, or **Bursa Kebabı** (*boorsa kebabuh*) – mild.

Balık Lokantası (*baluhk lokantassuh*): fish restaurants which can be found at port cities, and especially along the Bosphorus in Istanbul. They merit a visit not only for the fresh seafood and the rich selection of hors d'oeuvres, **meze**, they serve, but also for the general merriment that results from the **rakı** (*rakuh*) traditionally drunk with such food.

İşkembeci (*eesh-kembejee*): the Turkish equivalent of the fish and chip shop, offering cheap and nourishing food. However, they are definitely not for the faint-hearted as they specialize in all types of offal and excel in tripe soup, which gives them their name.

Muhallebici (*muhal-lebeejee*): these are usually clean, pleasant places serving a rich variety of puddings. They also offer a clear chicken soup, chicken and rice, and are often used by Turks for a light lunch.

Kahve (*hahveh*) or **kahvehane** (*kahveh-haneh*): this is a coffee shop where, traditionally, men sit playing **tavla** (backgammon) and drinking tea, coffee, and soft drinks. The **çay bahçesi** (*ch-'eye'-bahchehsee*) is a more suitable place for families.

These usually have tables and chairs outside where you can sit and buy tea by the cup or by the samovar, **semaver** (*semaver*). You can also have coffee or soft drinks and will be allowed to eat your own food.

Finally, a host of restaurants on pushcarts, some quite elaborate affairs, which mainly serve one type of food, congregate at crowded spots. Although the food they serve is often very tasty, their standards of hygiene are the subject of many jokes among the Turks and you should consider the risk before venturing to try them.

USEFUL WORDS AND PHRASES

beer	bira	*beera*
bill	hesap	*hessap*
bottle	şişe	*sheesheh*
bowl	kase	*ka-seh*
cake	pasta	*pasta*
chef	şef, aşçı	*shef, ash-chuh*
coffee	kahve	*kah-veh*
cup	fincan	*feenjan*
fork	çatal	*chatal*
glass	bardak	*bardak*
knife	bıçak	*buh-chak*
menu	yemek listesi	*yemek leestessee*
milk	süt	*sewt*
plate	tabak	*tabak*
receipt	makbuz	*makbooz*
sandwich	sandviç	*sand-veech*
serviette	peçete	*pecheteh*
snack	hafif yemek	*hafeef yemek*
soup	çorba	*chorba*
spoon	kaşık	*kashuhk*
sugar	şeker	*sheker*
table	masa	*massa*
tea	çay	*ch-'eye'*

teaspoon	çay kaşığı	*ch-'eye' kassuh-uh*
tip	bahşiş	*bah-sheesh*
waiter/waitress	garson	*garson*
water	su	*soo*
wine	şarap	*sharap*
wine list	şarap listesi	*sharap leesteesee*

A table for one/two, please
bir/iki kişilik bir masa, lütfen
beer/eekee keeshee-leek beer massa, lewtfen

Can we see the menu/wine list?
Yemek/şarap listesini görebilir miyiz?
yemek/sharap leestesseenee gureh-beeleer mee-yeez

Is this suitable for vegetarians?
Vejeteryanlar bunu yiyebilir mi?
vejeteryanlar boonoo yeeyebeeleer mee

What would you recommend?
Ne tavsiye edersiniz?
neh tav-see-yeh eder-seeneez

Do you do children's portions?
Çocuk porsiyonu veriyor musunuz?
chojook porseeyonoo vereeyor moosoonooz

I'd like …
… istiyorum
… *eesteeyoroom*

Just a cup of coffee, please
Yalnız bir fincan kahve, lütfen
yalnuhz beer feenjan kah-veh, lewtfen

Waiter/waitress!
Garson!
garson

Can we have the bill, please?
Hesabı getirir misiniz, lütfen?
hessabuh gheeteereer mee-seeneez, lewtfen

I only want a snack
Yalnız hafif bir şey istiyorum
yalnuhz hafeef beer shay eesteeyoroom

Is there a set menu?
Tabldot var mı?
tabldot var muh

I didn't order this
Ben bunu ısmarlamadım
ben boonoo uhss-marlamaduhm

May we have some more ...?
Biraz daha ... rica ediyoruz
beeraz daha ... reeja edeeyorooz

The meal was very good, thank you
Yemek çok iyiydi, teşekkür ederiz
yemek chock ee-yee-dee, teshek-kewr edereez

THINGS YOU'LL HEAR

Afiyet olsun
Enjoy your meal

MENU GUIDE

Adana kebabı	spicy hot meatballs
ahududu	raspberries
alabalık	trout
ananas	pineapple
ançüez	anchovies
armut	pears
Arnavut ciğeri	'Albanian' spicy fried liver with onions
aşure	'Noah's pudding' – a dessert with wheat grains, nuts and dried fruit
ayran	yoghurt drink
ayva	quince
ayva jölesi	quince jelly
ayva reçeli	quince jam
az pişmiş	rare
az şekerli kahve	slightly sweetened Turkish coffee
badem	almonds
badem kurabiyesi	almond cakes
badempare	almond cakes in syrup
badem tatlısı	almond cakes
bakla	broad beans
baklava	pastry filled with nuts and syrup
bal	honey
balık	fish
balık buğulaması	fish baked with tomatoes
balık çorbası	fish and lemon soup
balık kızartması	fried fish
balık köftesi	fish balls
bamya	okra
barbunya	red mullet
barbunya pilakisi	dried beans cooked in olive oil and served hot or cold
barbunya tava	fried mullet
bazlama	flat bread cooked on a hot-plate
beyaz peynir	white cheese
beyaz peynirli makarna	noodles with white cheese
beyaz şarap	white wine
beyin salatası	brain salad
bezelye	green peas
bıldırcın	quail

biber	peppers
biber dolması	stuffed green peppers
biftek	steak
bira	beer
bisküvi	biscuits
bonfile	fillet steak
boza	thick fermented grain drink
böbrek	kidneys
böbrek ızgara	grilled kidney
böbrek sote	sautéed kidneys
börek	layered pastry with cheese/meat/spinach filling
buğulama	steamed, poached
bulgur pilavı	cracked wheat cooked with tomatoes
Bursa kebabı	grilled lamb on pitta bread with tomato sauce and yoghurt
buz	ice
buzlu	with ice
bülbül yuvası	dessert with nuts and syrup
cacık	chopped cucumber in garlic flavoured yoghurt
ceviz	walnuts
ciğer	liver
ciğer sarması	minced liver wrapped in lambs' fat
ciğer tava	fried liver
cin	gin
cintonik	gin and tonic
çam fıstığı	pine nuts
çavdar ekmeği	rye bread
çay	tea
Çerkez tavuğu	'Circassian' cold chicken in walnut sauce with garlic
çılbır	poached eggs with yoghurt
çiğ köfte	raw meatballs: a dish made of minced meat, pounded wheat and chilli powder
çikolata	chocolate
çikolatalı	with chocolate
çikolatalı dondurma	chocolate ice cream
çikolatalı pasta	chocolate cake
çilek	strawberry
çilekli dondurma	strawberry ice cream

çilek reçeli	strawberry jam
çips	crisps
çiroz	salted dried mackerel
çoban salatası	mixed tomatoes, peppers, cucumbers and onion salad
çok pişmiş	well-done
çok şekerli kahve	very sweet Turkish coffee
çorba	soup
çöp kebabı	small pieces of lamb baked on wooden spits
çörek	kind of bun
çulluk	woodcock
dana eti	veal
dana rozbif	roast veal
deniz ürünleri	seafood
dereotu	dill
dil	ox tongue
dil balığı	sole
dilber dudağı	lip-shaped sweet pastry with nut filling
dolma	stuffed vegetables (with or without meat)
domates	tomatoes
domatesli	with tomatoes
domatesli pilav	rice cooked with tomatoes
domatesli pirinç çorbası	rice and tomato soup
domates salatası	tomato salad
domates salçalı patlıcan kızartması	fried aubergines with tomato and garlic sauce
domates salçası	tomato sauce
domates suyu	tomato juice
dondurma	ice cream
döner kebap	lamb grilled on a spit and served in thin slices, usually with rice and salad
dut	mulberries
düğün çorbası	'wedding' soup made of meat stock, yoghurt and egg
ekmek	bread
ekmek kadayıfı	sweet pastry
ekşi	sour
elma	apples
elma suyu	apple juice
elma tatlısı	dessert made with apples
enginar	artichokes

erik	plums
erişte	homemade noodles
et	meat
etli	with meat
etli Ayşe kadın	meat with green beans
etli bezelye	pea stew
etli biber dolması	peppers stuffed with rice and meat
etli bulgur pilavı	cracked wheat with meat
etli domates dolması	tomatoes stuffed with meat and rice
etli kabak dolması	marrows stuffed with meat and rice
etli kapuska	cabbage stew with meat
etli kuru fasulye	lamb and haricot beans in tomato sauce
etli lahana dolması	cabbage leaves stuffed with meat and rice
etli nohut	chickpea and meat stew
etli yaprak dolması	vine leaves stuffed with rice and meat
et suyu	meat stock
ezme(si)	purée
eno gulin çorbası	lentil and rice soup
fasulye	beans
fasulye pilaki	beans in olive oil
fasulye piyazı	beans and onion salad
fava	broad bean purée
fındık	hazelnuts
fırın	baked, oven-roasted
fırında	baked, oven-roasted
fıstık	peanuts
fıstıklı	with pistachio nuts
fıstıklı dondurma	ice cream with pistachio nuts
fıstıklı muhallebi	rice flour and rosewater pudding with pistachio nuts
füme	smoked
gazoz	fizzy drink
greypfrut	grapefruit
güllaç	rice wafers stuffed with nuts, cooked in milk
gümüş	silverfish
güveç	meat and vegetable stew
güvercin	pigeon
hamsi	anchovy
hanım parmağı	'Lady's Fingers' – dried dough-sticks in syrup
hardal	mustard
haşlama	boiled, stewed

haşlanmış yumurta	boiled egg
havuç	carrots
havuç salatası	shredded carrot salad
havyar	caviar
hazır yemek	ready-to-eat food
helva	general name for various sweets made from cereals, nuts, sesame oil and honey
hıyar	cucumber
hindi	turkey
hindiba	wild chicory
hindi dolması	stuffed turkey
hindistan cevizi	coconut
hoşaf	stewed fruit
hurma	dates
hünkar beğendi	'Sultan's Delight' – lamb served with aubergine purée
ıhlamur	lime-blossom tea
ıspanak	spinach
ıspanaklı börek	spinach wrapped in thin pastry
ıspanaklı yumurta	eggs with spinach
ıstakoz	lobster
ızgara	grilled
ızgara balık	grilled fish
ızgara köfte	grilled meatballs
içecek	beverage
içki	alcoholic drink
içli köfte	meatballs stuffed with cracked wheat
iç pilav	rice with currants, pine nuts and onions
imam bayıldı	split aubergines with tomatoes and onions, eaten cold with olive oil
incir	figs
irmik helvası	semolina **helva**
İskender kebabı	grilled lamb on pitta bread with tomato sauce and yoghurt
islim kebabı	steamed kebab
istiridye	oysters
işkembe çorbası	tripe soup
iyi pişmiş	well-done, well-cooked
jambon	ham
kabak	courgettes, pumpkin, marrow
kabak dolması	stuffed courgettes

kabak kızartması	fried marrows
kabak reçeli	marrow jam
kabak tatlısı	pumpkin with syrup and walnuts
kadın budu köfte	'Lady's Thighs' – meat and rice croquettes
kadın göbeği	'Lady's Navel' – flour and egg-based fried dessert soaked in syrup
kağıt kebabı	lamb and vegetables in paper
kağıtta barbunya	red mullet grilled in paper wrapping
kağıtta pişmiş	baked in paper
kahve	coffee
kakao	cocoa
kalkan	turbot
kanyak	brandy
kara biber	black pepper
karadut	black mulberries
karagöz	black bream
kara zeytin	black olives
karışık	mixed
karışık dondurma	mixed ice cream
karışık ızgara	mixed grill
karışık salata	mixed salad
karides	prawns
karides tavası	prawns fried in batter
karnabahar	cauliflower
karnıyarık	split aubergines with meat filling
karpuz	watermelon
kaşar peyniri	mild yellow cheese
kaşar peynirli makarna	noodles with kaşar cheese
kavun	honey-dew melon
kavunlu dondurma	melon ice cream
kayısı	apricots
kayısı reçeli	apricot jam
kayısı suyu	apricot juice
kaymak	clotted cream
kaymaklı	with clotted cream
kaymaklı dondurma	dairy ice cream
kaz	goose
kazan dibi	pudding with a caramel base
kebap	roast meat
kefal	grey mullet

MENU GUIDE

kefal pilakisi	mullet cooked in olive oil with vegetables
kek	cake
keklik	partridge
kereviz	celery
kestane	chestnuts
kestane şekeri	marrons glacés, candied chestnuts
keşkek	lamb with cracked wheat
keşkül	almond pudding
kılıç (balığı)	swordfish
kılıç ızgara	grilled swordfish
kılıç şiş	swordfish on skewers
kırmızı biber	paprika
kırmızı mercimek çorbası	red lentil soup
kırmızı şarap	red wine
kısır	cracked wheat and paprika
kış türlüsü	stewed winter vegetables
kıyma	minced meat
kıymalı	with minced meat
kıymalı bamya	okra with minced meat
kıymalı ıspanak	spinach with minced meat
kıymalı karnabahar	cauliflower with minced meat
kıymalı makarna	noodles with minced meat
kıymalı mercimek	meat and lentils
kıymalı pide	pitta bread with meat filling
kıymalı yumurta	eggs with minced meat
kızarmış ekmek	toast
kızartma	fried, broiled
kiraz	cherries
koç yumurtası	'rams' eggs' – a delicacy made from rams' testicles
kokoreç	lambs' intestines grilled on a spit
komposto	cold stewed fruit
koyun eti	mutton
köfte	meatballs or patties
köpüklü şarap	sparkling wine
krema	cream
kremalı pasta	cream cake
krem karamel	crème caramel
kurabiye	cake with almonds or nuts
kuru	dried
kuru fasulye	haricot beans in tomato sauce

kuru köfte	fried meatballs
kuru üzüm	raisins
kuru yemiş	dried fruit and nuts
kuskus pilavı	cous-cous – cooked semolina, usually served with meat
kuşbaşı	small pieces of casseroled meat
kuşkonmaz	asparagus
kuzu eti	lamb
kuzu fırında	roast leg of lamb
kuzu kapama	lamb with lettuce
kuzu pirzolası	grilled lamb chops
lahana	cabbage
lahana dolması	stuffed cabbage leaves
lahana turşusu	pickled cabbage
lahmacun	pancakes with spicy meat filling
leblebi	small chickpeas
levrek	sea bass
likör	liqueur
limon	lemon
limonata	still lemon drink
limonlu dondurma	lemon ice cream
lokum	Turkish Delight
lüfer	bluefish
maden suyu	mineral water
makarna	macaroni, noodles
mandalina	tangerines
mantar	mushrooms
mantı	type of ravioli
marmelat	jam
marul	cos lettuce
maydanoz	parsley
mayonezli balık	fish with mayonnaise
menba suyu	spring water
menemen	omelette with tomatoes and peppers
mercan	bream
mercimek	lentils
mercimek çorbası	lentil soup
mersin balığı	sturgeon
meşrubat	soft drinks
meyva suyu	fruit juice
meze	hors d'oeuvres

mısır	corn
midye	mussels
midye dolması	stuffed mussels
midyeli pilav	rice with mussels
midye pilakisi	mussels cooked in oil with vegetables
midye tavası	fried mussels
muhallebi	rice flour and rosewater pudding
musakka	moussaka
muska böreği	triangles of pastry filled with cheese, parsley etc
muz	banana
mücver	vegetable patties
nane	mint
nar	pomegranate
nemse böreği	meat pie with puff pastry
neskafe	any brand of instant coffee
nohut	cooked chickpeas
nohutlu paça	lambs' feet with chickpeas
nohutlu yahni	lamb and chickpeas
omlet	omelette
orta pişmiş	medium
orta şekerli kahve	medium sweet Turkish coffee
ördek	duck
paça	lambs' feet
paça çorbası	lambs' feet soup
palamut	tunny
pancar	beetroot
pancar turşusu	pickled beetroot
papatya çayı	camomile tea
paskalya çöreği	Easter bread – slightly sweetened bread in a plait
pasta	cake
pastırma	cumin and garlic cured beef
pastırmalı yumurta	fried eggs with **pastırma**
patates	potatoes
patates köftesi	potato and cheese balls
patates kızartması	chips
patatesli	with potatoes
patates püresi	creamed potatoes
patates salatası	potato salad
patlıcan	aubergines

patlıcan dolma turşusu	pickled stuffed aubergines
patlıcan kebabı	aubergine wrapped round pieces of meat and roasted
patlıcan kızartması	fried aubergines
patlıcanlı pilav	rice with aubergines
patlıcan salatası	aubergine purée
pavurya	crab
pembe şarap	rosé wine
peynir	cheese
peynirli	with cheese
peynirli omlet	cheese omelette
peynirli pide	cheese pitta bread
peynirli tepsi böreği	cheese pie
peynir tatlısı	small cheese-cakes in syrup
pırasa	leek
pide	pitta bread
pilaki	cold white beans in vinaigrette
pilav	rice cooked in butter
pilavlı tavuk	chicken and rice
piliç	chicken
piliç ızgarası	grilled chicken
pirinç	rice (uncooked)
pirzola	lamb chops
pisi	plaice
pişkin	well-cooked
piyaz	haricot bean salad
poğaça	pastries with meat or cheese filling
portakal	oranges
portakal reçeli	orange jam
portakal suyu	orange juice
puf böreği	meat or cheese pasties
püre	purée
rafadan	soft-boiled egg
rakı	Turkish national drink, distilled from grape juice and aniseed-flavoured
reçel	jam
revani	sweet semolina pastry
roka	kind of watercress
rom	rum
rosto	roasted
rus salatası	Russian salad – mayonnaise, peas, carrots etc

sade kahve	Turkish coffee without sugar
sade pilav	plain rice **pilav**
sahanda yumurta	fried eggs
salam	salami
salata	salad
salatalık	cucumber
salça	tomato sauce or paste
salçalı	with tomato sauce
salçalı köfte	meatballs in tomato sauce
salep	drink made from **salep** root in hot milk and cinnamon
salyangoz	snails
sandviç ekmeği	rolls
saray lokması	fried batter dipped in syrup
sardalya	sardines
sarığı burma	'Twisted Turban' – turban-shaped **baklava**
sarmısak	garlic
sazan	carp
sebze	vegetables
sebze çorbası	vegetable soup
sek şarap	dry wine
semizotu	purslane – a herb mixed in salads or stewed
sıcak	hot, warm
sığır eti	beef
sigara böreği	cigarette-shaped fried pastry filled with cheese, parsley etc
simit	ring-shaped bread covered with sesame seeds
sirke	vinegar
soda	soda water
soğan	onions
soğan dolması	stuffed onions
soğuk	cold
sombalığı	salmon
sos	sauce
sosis	sausage
soslu	with sauce
su	water
su böreği	layered pastry
sucuk	Turkish sausage with spices and garlic
sumak	sumac – a herb eaten with kebabs
su muhallebisi	rice-flour pudding with rosewater

supanglez	mousse – plain or chocolate
sülün	pheasant
süt	milk
sütlaç	rice pudding
sütlü	with milk
sütlü kahve	coffee with milk
süzme yoğurt	strained yoghurt
şalgam	turnip
şam fıstığı	pistachio nuts
şam tatlısı	dessert with syrup
şarap	wine
şeftali	peaches
şeftali reçeli	peach jam
şeftali suyu	peach juice
şehriye	vermicelli
şehriye çorbası	vermicelli soup with lemon
şehriyeli	with vermicelli
şehriyeli pilav	pilav with vermicelli
şeker	sugar
şekerli	with sugar
şekerpare	small cakes with syrup
şerbet	sweetened and iced fruit juices
şıra	grape juice
şiş	cooked on a skewer
şişe	bottle
şiş kebabı	small pieces of lamb grilled on skewers
şiş köfte	grilled meatballs on skewers
şurup	syrup
talaş kebabı	lamb baked in pastry
tarama	roe pâté
tarator	nut and garlic sauce
taratorlu karnabahar	cauliflower with nut and garlic sauce
tarhana çorbası	traditional soup with dried yoghurt, tomato and pimento
tas kebabı	diced lamb with rice
tatar böreği	ravioli
tatlı	sweet, dessert
tatlı şarap	sweet wine
tava(da)	fried
tavşan	rabbit
tavuk	chicken

tavuk çorbası	chicken soup
tavuk göğsü	chicken breast pudding – a dessert
tavuk ızgara	barbecued chicken
tavuklu pilav	chicken and rice
taze	fresh
taze beyaz peynir	fresh white cheese
taze fasulye	runner beans in tomato sauce and olive oil
taze soğan	spring onions
tekir	striped mullet
tel kadayıfı	shredded wheat stuffed with nuts in syrup
terbiye	egg and lemon sauce
terbiyeli	with egg and lemon sauce
terbiyeli haşlama	boiled lamb with egg and lemon sauce
terbiyeli köfte	meatballs with egg and lemon sauce
tereyağı	butter
torik	large tunny
tost	toasted sandwich
tulumba tatlısı	semolina doughnut in syrup
tulum peyniri	goat's milk cheese made in a skin
turna	pike
turp	radish
turşu	pickled vegetables
turşu suyu	juice of pickled vegetables
turunç	Seville oranges
tuz	salt
tuzlu	salty
tükenmez	a soft drink of mixed fruit
türlü	meat and vegetable stew
un helvası	flour **helva**
uskumru	mackerel
uskumru dolması	stuffed mackerel
üzüm	grapes
vanilya	vanilla
viski	whisky
vişne	black cherries
vişne suyu	black cherry juice
votka	vodka
yağ	oil, fat
yahni	meat stew with onions
yaprak dolması	stuffed vine leaves
yayla çorbası	yoghurt soup

yaz türlüsü	stewed summer vegetables
yengeç	crab
yerfıstığı	peanuts
yeşil mercimek çorbası	green lentil soup
yeşil salata	green salad
yeşil zeytin	green olives
yoğurt	yoghurt
yoğurtlu	with yoghurt
yoğurtlu kebap	kebab with pitta bread and yoghurt
yoğurtlu paça	lambs' feet with yoghurt and garlic
yumurta	egg
yumurtalı	with egg
zerde	saffron rice dessert
zeytin	olives
zeytinyağı	olive oil
zeytinyağlı	in olive oil (eaten cold)
zeytinyağlı biber dolması	stuffed sweet peppers in olive oil
zeytinyağlı enginar	artichokes in olive oil
zeytinyağlı kereviz	celery in olive oil
zeytinyağlı patlıcan pilavı	rice with aubergines in olive oil
zeytinyağlı pırasa	leeks in olive oil
zeytinyağlı pilaki	red haricot beans in olive oil
zeytinyağlı taze bakla	fresh broad beans in olive oil
zeytinyağlı yaprak dolması	vine leaves stuffed with rice, pine nuts and raisins
zeytinyağlı yeşil fasulye	runner beans cooked in tomatoes and olive oil

SHOPPING

Although the official opening hours for shops are from 9 am to 7 pm, Monday to Saturday, it is quite possible, particularly in small towns, to find shops open seven days a week, from early morning till late at night. The numerous grocery stores, **bakkal** (*bak-kal*), tend to have long opening hours everywhere and sell a variety of goods apart from basic food stuffs.

While bargaining is acceptable in some shops, it is not usual if the goods already have a price tag or if a sign such as **Pazarlık edilmez** (*pazarluhk edeel-mez*) is displayed. This means 'no bargaining'. However, when it comes to the markets, for which Turkey is justly famous, it is always advisable to bargain and to shop around, asking prices. Tourists are often invited to drink tea, coffee or soft drinks by the shopkeeper, but this does not put them under any obligation to buy. Bargaining is not a fast process and it is important not to try to hurry proceedings, nor is it advisable to show too much eagerness to buy. Indeed, walking out of the shop may result in a better offer from the shopkeeper.

Foreign books and newspapers can be bought at specialist bookshops, called **kitapçı** (*keetap-chuh*) or **kitabevi** (*keetab-evee*); Turkish newspapers are sold in grocery stores and on newsstands.

Useful Words and Phrases

baker	fırın	*fuhrun*
bargaining	pazarlık	*pazarluhk*
bazaar	pazar, çarşı	*pazar, charshuh*
bookshop	kitapçı	*keetap-chuh*
butcher	kasap	*kassap*
to buy	satın almak	*satuhn almak*
cake shop	pastane	*pastaneh*
carpet	halı	*haluh*
chemist	eczane	*ez-za-neh*
department store	büyük mağaza	*bew-yewk ma-aza*
fashion	moda	*moda*

fishmonger	balıkçı	*baluhk-chuh*
florist	çiçekçi	*cheechek-chee*
grocer	bakkal	*bak-kal*
ironmonger	nalbur	*nalboor*
market	pazar, çarşı	*pazar, charshuh*
menswear	erkek giyim eşyası	*erkek ghee-yeem esh-yasuh*
newsagent	gazete bayii	*gazeh-teh ba-yee*
off-licence	tekel bayii	*tekel ba-yee*
pharmacy	eczane	*ez-za-neh*
receipt	makbuz	*makbooz*
record shop	plakçı	*plak-chuh*
sale	satış	*satuhsh*
shoe shop	ayakkabıcı	*'eye'-yak-kabuh juh*
shop	dükkan	*dewk-kan*
to go shopping	alışverişe çıkmak	*aluhsh-vereesheh chuhk-mak*
souvenir shop	turistik eşya dukkanı	*tooreesteek esh-ya dewk kan nuh*
special offer	özel indirim	*urzel eendeercem*
to spend	harcamak	*harjamak*
stationer	kırtasiyeci	*kuhr-tassee-yeh-jee*
supermarket	süpermarket	*sewpermarket*
tailor	terzi	*terzee*
till	kasa	*kassa*
toyshop	oyuncakçı	*oyoon-jak-chuh*
travel agent	seyahat acentesi	*sayahat ajentessee*
women's wear	kadın gıyim eşyası	*kaduhn ghee-yeem esh-yasuh*

Can you help me?
Bakar mısınız?
bakar muh-suh-nuhz

I'd like ...
... istiyorum
... *eesteeyoroom*

Do you have ...?
... var mı?
... *var muh*

How much is this?
Bu kaç lira?
boo kach leera

Where is the ... department?
... bölümü nerede?
... *burlewmew neh-reh-deh*

Do you have any more of these?
Bunlardan başka var mı?
boonlardan bashka var muh

Have you anything cheaper?
Daha ucuz bir şey var mı?
daha ooj-ooz beer shay var muh

Have you anything larger?
Daha büyüğü var mı?
daha bew-yew-ew var muh

Have you anything smaller?
Daha küçüğü var mı?
daha kew-chew-ew var muh

Does it come in other colours?
Başka renkleri var mı?
bashka renkleree var muh

Can I try it/them on?
Üstümde deneyebilir miyim?
ewss-tewm-deh deneh-ych beeleer mee-yeem

Where do I pay?
Kasa nerede?
kassa neh-reh-deh

Can I have a refund?
Paramı geri alabilir miyim?
paramuh gheree alabeeleer mee-yeem

I'm just looking
Şöyle bir bakıyorum
shurleh beer bakuh-yoroom

I'll come back later
Sonra tekrar geleceğim
sonra tekrar ghel-ejeh-eem

That's far too much
Çok pahalı
chok pahaluh

I'll give you ...
Size ... vereyim
seezeh ... vereh-yeem

That's my last offer
Daha fazla veremem
daha fazla vereh-mem

OK, I'll take it
Tamam, alıyorum
tamam, aluh-yoroom

Could you wrap it for me?
Lütfen paket yapar mısınız?
lewtfen paket yapar muh-suh-nuhz?

Can I have a receipt?
Bir makbuz rica ediyorum
beer makbooz reeja edeeyoroom

Can I have a bag, please?
Bir torba rica ediyorum
beer torba reeja edeeyoroom

THINGS YOU'LL HEAR

Yardım edebilir miyim?
Can I help you?

Daha aşağı olmaz
That's my final offer

Üstünüzde denemek ister misiniz?
Would you like to try it on?

Maalesef mevcudu tükendi
I'm sorry, we're out of stock

Para iade etmiyoruz
We cannot give cash refunds

Bir alacak pusulası verebilirim
I can give you a credit note

→

Mevcut mallarımız bu kadar
That is all we have

Bozuk para rica edeceğim
Have you got anything smaller? (money)

Özür dilerim, onu bozamayacağım
Sorry, I've no change for that note

Buyurun
Please/Do come in/Go ahead etc

Güle güle giy!/Güle güle kullan!
means Wear it happily/Use it happily (said by shopkeepers
   when you make a purchase)

THINGS YOU'LL SEE

antika	antiques
ayakkabı	shoes
aylık taksitler	monthly instalments
bakkaliye	groceries
bölüm	department
büro malzemeleri	office supplies
büyük mağaza	department store
çay	tea
depozito	deposit
dergi	magazine
düzine	dozen
fiyat	price
gazete	newspaper
halılar	carpets
içki	spirits
indirimli satış	sale (reduced prices)
kadın giyim eşyası	women's clothes

→

kafetarya	snackbar
kahve	coffee
kalite	quality
kaliteli	high quality
kapalı çarşı	covered bazaar
kasap	butcher
kasap dükkanı	butcher's shop
kilim	rug
kilogram	kilogram
kira	rental
kitabevi, kitapçı	bookshop
kürk	fur
mallar	goods
moda	fashion
oyuncaklar	toys
özel fiyat	special price
özel indirim	special offer
pastane	cake shop
pazarlık edilmez	no bargaining
satılan mal makbuzu olmadan değiştirilmez	goods are not exchanged without receipt
satın alma	purchase
satış	sale
şekerleme	confectionery
selfservis	self-service
seyahat acentesi	travel agent
tütüneü	tobacconist
taksitler	instalments
tatlı yiyecekler	confectionery
tükendi	sold out
ucuz	inexpensive
üst kat	upper floor

AT THE HAIRDRESSER

Turkish hairdressers are similar to those found in most
European countries. A range of beauty treatments may also be
offered at some women's hairdressers.

USEFUL WORDS AND PHRASES

appointment	randevu	randeh voo
beard	sakal	sakal
bleach	rengini açmak	ren-gheenee ach-mak
blond	sarışın	saruh-shuhn
brush	fırça	fuhr-cha
comb	tarak	turuk
conditioner	balsam, saç kremi	balsam, sach kremee
curlers	bigudi	beegoodee
curling tongs	saç maşası	sach masha-suh
curly	kıvırcık	kuh-vuhr-juhk
dark	koyu renk	koyoo renk
fringe	kakül	ka-kewl
gel	jel	jel
hair	saç	sach
haircut	saç tıraşı	sach tuhrashuh
(for women)	saç kesme	sach kess-meh
hairdresser	berber	berber
(for women)	kuaför	kwaffur
hairdryer	saç kurutma makinesi	sach koorootma makeenessee
highlights	meç	mech
long	uzun	oozoon
moustache	bıyık	buh-yuhk
parting	ayırma	'eye'-yuhr-ma
perm	perma	perma
shampoo	şampuan	shampooan
shave	sakal tıraşı	sakal tuhrash-uh
shaving foam	tıraş köpüğü	tuhrash kur-pew-ew
short	kısa	kuh-sa

75

styling mousse	saç kremi	*sach kremee*
tint	hafif boya	*hafeef boya*
wavy	dalgalı	*dalgaluh*

I'd like to make an appointment
Randevu almak istiyorum
randeh-voo almak eesteeyoroom

Just a trim, please
Lütfen yalnız uçlarından biraz alın
lewtfen yalnuhz ooch-laruhndan beeraz aluhn

Not too much off, please
Lütfen fazla kısaltmayın
lewtfen fazla kuh-saltm-'eye'-yuhm

A bit more off here, please
Lütfen burasını biraz daha kısaltın
lewtfen boora-suhnuh beeraz daha kuh-saltuhn

I'd like a cut and blow-dry
Lütfen kesip fönle kurutun
lewtfen kesseep furnleh koorootoon

I'd like a perm
Perma yaptırmak istiyorum
perma yaptuhr-mak eesteeyoroom

I'd like highlights
Meç istiyorum
mech eesteeyoroom

THINGS YOU'LL SEE OR HEAR

arkadan	at the back
ayırma	parting
bahşiş	tip
berber	men's hairdresser
bukle	curl
daha kısa	shorter
enseden	back of the neck
fönle kurutma	blow-dry
jilet	razor blade
kesmek	to cut
kısa	short
kuaför	women's hairdresser
kuru	dry
mizanpli	set
önden	at the front
perçem	fringe
perma	perm
sakal	beard
tıraş köpüğü	shaving foam
tıraş sabunu	shaving soap
ton vermek	tint
uzun	long
yan	side
yıkamak	to wash

SPORT

The long coastline and very favourable weather conditions provide excellent opportunities for water sports in the summer. Swimming, water-skiing, sailing, and sailboarding are all available. Skin diving is a popular sport, not least because the Western Aegean coast is full of sunken cities and other marvels. However, a word of caution is necessary with regard to any historical relics you may find: it is illegal to take them out of Turkey.

In the winter, skiing is possible in several locations, the most popular of which is Mount Olympus (Uludağ) near Istanbul. There are also many unspoilt mountains and forests for walking and mountaineering. Foreigners may join hunting parties organized by specialist travel agencies, which will provide all the necessary information concerning permits, seasons, weapons and ammunition.

Finally, for those who would rather watch a unique spectacle, there is the traditional Turkish sport of oil wrestling. The wrestlers are covered in olive oil which makes it difficult for the opponents to get a hold on each other. Every July wrestling championships are held in Kırkpınar outside Edirne.

USEFUL WORDS AND PHRASES

athletics	atletizm	*atleteezm*
badminton	badminton	*badmeenton*
ball	top	*top*
beach	plaj	*plaj*
bicycle	bisiklet	*beesseeklet*
canoe	kano	*kano*
deck chair	şezlong	*shezlong*
to dive	dalmak	*dalmak*
diving board	tramplen	*tramplen*
fishing	balık avlama	*baluhk avlama*
fishing rod	olta kamışı	*olta kamuhshuh*

football	futbol	footbol
football match	futbol maçı	footbol machuh
golf	golf	golf
golf course	golf sahası	golf sahassuh
gymnastics	jimnastik	jeemnasteek
hunting	avcılık	av-juhluhk
jogging	koşu	koshoo
lake	göl	gurl
racket	raket	raket
riding	binicilik	beeneejeeleek
rowing boat	kayık	k-'eye'-yuhk
to run	koşmak	koshmak
sailboard	yelkenli sörf	yelkenlee surf
sailing	yelkencilik	yelkenjeeleek
sand	kum	koom
sea	deniz	deneez
skiing	kayak	k-'eye'-yak
sledge	kızak	kuhzak
snorkel	şnorkel	shnorkel
snow	kar	kar
stadium	stadyum	stad-yoom
to swim	yüzmek	yewzmek
swimming pool	yüzme havuzu	yewzeh havoozoo
tennis	tenis	teneess
tennis court	tenis kortu	teneess kortoo
tennis racket	tenis raketi	teneess raketee
tent	çadır	chaduhr
Turkish wrestling	yağlı güreş	ya-luh ghewresh
volleyball	voleybol	voleybol
walking	yürüyüş	yewrew-yewsh
water-skiing	su kayağı	soo k-'eye'-ya-uh
water-skis	su kayağı	soo k-'eye'-ya-uh
wave	dalga	dalga
winter sports	kış sporları	kuhsh sporlaruh
yacht	yat	yat

How do I get to the beach?
Plaja nereden gidilir?
plaja neh-reh-den gheedeeleer

How deep is the water here?
Burada suyun derinliği ne kadar?
boorada soo-yoon dereenlee-ee neh kadar

Is there an indoor/outdoor pool here?
Burada kapalı/açık havuz var mı?
boorada kapaluh/achuhk havooz var muh

Is it safe to swim here?
Burada güvenle yüzülebilir mi?
boorada ghew-venleh yewzewleh-beeleer mee

Can I fish here?
Burada balık tutabilir miyim?
boorada baluhk tootabeeleer mee-yeem

Do I need a licence?
İzin belgesi lazım mı?
eezeen belghessee la-zuhm muh

I would like to hire a bike
Bir bisiklet kiralamak istiyorum
beer beesseeklet keeralamak eesteeyoroom

How much does it cost per hour/day?
Bir saatlik/günlük kirası ne kadar?
beer sa-atleek/ghewnlewk keerassuh neh kadar

Where can I hire ...?
Nerede ... kiralayabilirim?
neh-reh-deh ... keeral-'eye'-yabeeleereem

Things You'll See or Hear

açık yüzme havuzu	open-air swimming pool
avcılık	hunting
balık tutmak yasaktır	no fishing
bisikletçi	cyclist
dağcılık	mountaineering
dalmak	to dive
dalma techizatı	skin diving equipment
girmek yasaktır	no entry, keep out
ilk yardım	first aid
kapalı yüzme havuzu	indoor swimming pool
kar	snow
kayak yapmak	skiing
kiralık bisiklet	bicycle hire
kiralık kayık	boat hire
kürek çekmek	to row
liman	port
marina	marina
orman	forest
spor tesisleri	sports facilities
su kayağı	water-skiing
su sporları	water sports
tehlike	danger
tehlikeli akıntı	dangerous current
yağlı güreş	oil wrestling
yasak	forbidden
yelkencilik	sailing
yelkenli	sailing boat
yürümek	to walk
yürüyüş	walking
yüzmek	to swim
yüzmek yasaktır	no swimming

POST OFFICES AND BANKS

Post offices are generally open from 8.30 am until 5.30 pm, Monday to Friday, but close for one hour at noon. Main post offices stay open until late into the night and maintain a skeleton service on Saturdays and Sundays. They are easily recognizable by their yellow **PTT** signs. Post restante facilities are available at main (**Merkez**) post offices. Letter boxes in Turkey are painted yellow.

Most banks are open from 8.30 am to midday and from 1.30 to 5.00 pm, Monday to Friday, although some are open on Saturdays. The basic unit of Turkish currency is the **Lira**. The symbol for it, TL, is placed after the amount, eg 50,000TL.

USEFUL WORDS AND PHRASES

airmail	uçak postası	*oochak postassuh*
bank	banka	*banka*
banknote	banknot	*banknot*
to change	değiştirmek, bozmak	*deh-eeshteermek, bozmak*
cheque	çek	*chek*
collection	boşaltma	*boshaltma*
counter	gişe	*gheesheh*
customs forms	gümrük formüleri	*ghewm-rewk formewleree*
delivery	teslim	*tessleem*
exchange rate	döviz kuru	*durveez kooroo*
form	formüler	*formewler*
letter	mektup	*mektoop*
letter box	mektup kutusu	*mektoop kootoosoo*
mail	posta	*posta*
main post office	merkez postanesi	*merkez postanessee*
money order	havale	*havaleh*
package	paket	*paket*
parcel	koli	*kolee*
post	posta	*posta*

postage rates	posta ücretleri	*posta ewj-retleree*
postal order	posta havalesi	*posta havalessee*
postcard	posta kartı,	*posta kartuh,*
	kartpostal	*kartpostal*
postcode	posta kodu	*posta kodoo*
poste restante	postrestant	*post-restant*
postman	postacı	*postajuh*
post office	postane	*postaneh*
pound sterling	İngiliz Sterlını	*eengheeleez sterleenee*
registered letter	taahhütlü mektup	*ta-ah-hewtlew mektoop*
stamp	pul	*pool*
telephone	telefon	*telefon*
telephone box	telefon kabini	*telefon kabeenee*
token	jeton	*jeton*
traveller's cheque	seyahat çeki	*sayahat chekee*

How much is a letter to …?
…-e mektup ücreti ne kadar?
…-eh mektoop ewj-retee neh kadar

I would like to send a postcard to …
…-e bir kartpostal göndermek istiyorum
…-eh beer kartpostal gurn-dermek eesteeyoroom

I would like three 200,000 lira stamps
Üç adet 200,000 Liralık pul rica ediyorum
ewch adet eekee-yewz been leeraluhk pool reeja edeeyoroom

I want to register this letter
Bu mektubu taahhütlü göndermek istiyorum
boo mektooboo ta-ah-hewtlew gurn-dermek eesteeyoroom

I want to send this parcel to …
Bu koliyi …-e göndermek istiyorum
boo kolee-yee …-eh gurn-dermek eesteeyoroom

How long does the post to … take?
…-e ne kadar zamanda varır?
…-eh neh kadar zamanda varuhr

Where can I post this?
Bunu nereden postalayabilirim?
boonoo neh-reh-den postal-'eye'-ya-beeleereem

Is there any mail for me?
Bana mektup var mı?
bana mektoop var muh

This is to go airmail
Bu uçak postası ile gidecek
boo oochak postassuh eeleh gheedejek

I'd like to change this into lira
Bunu Türk Lirasına çevirmek istiyorum
boonoo tewrk leerassuhna cheveermek eesteeyoroom

Can I cash these traveller's cheques here?
Bu seyahat çeklerini burada bozdurabilir miyim?
boo sayahat cheklereenee boorada bozdoora- beeleer mee-yeem

What is the rate for the pound?
İngiliz Sterlininin kuru nedir?
eengheeleez sterleeneeneen kooroo nedeer

THINGS YOU'LL SEE

açık	open
adres	address
az miktarlarda pul	stamps in small quantities
banka	bank
cadde	street
çalışma saatleri	opening hours
doldurunuz	fill in
döviz (bürosu)	exchange, bureau de change
gişe	counter
gönderen	sender
gönderilen	addressee
havale	money order
ikamet adresi	domicile
kapalı	closed
kartpostal	postcard
kasa	cash desk
koli	parcel
koli gişesi	parcels counter
küçük paket	small packet
matbua	printed matter
mektup	letter
memur	official
merkez postanesi	central post office
müteakip boşaltma	next collection
numara	number (house)
otomatik arama	direct dialling
paket	packet, package
posta kartı	postcard
postane	post office
PTT	Post, Telephone and Telecommunications
pul	stamp
sokak	street
taahhütlü mektup	registered mail

$\longrightarrow$

telefon	telephone
telefon kabini	telephone box
telgraf	telegram
uçakla	airmail
uçak postası	airmail
yıldırım telgraf	express telegram
yurtdışı posta ücretleri	overseas postage rates
yurtiçi posta ücretleri	inland postal rate

THINGS YOU'LL HEAR

Pasaportunuzu görebilir miyim lütfen?
Can I see your passport, please?

Maalesef … kabul etmiyoruz
I'm afraid we don't accept …

COMMUNICATIONS

Telephones: The telephone system in Turkey is operated by a private company, **Türk Telekom**. Public telephones are usually blue. They tend to be few and far between and are generally found in the central areas of large cities. However, there are many public call boxes installed in small shops and restaurants which display a sign (**Telefon**). Public telephones are either cardphones or Jeton phones. phonecards can be bought in various values from post offices or kiosks. They are better for long-distance calls but there tend to be long queues at these phone boxes. **Jeton** are tokens and come in two sizes: small, and medium for long-distance calls; they can be bought in post offices. In addition, there are a few credit card phones in central Istanbul and Ankara and in some hotels.

Direct dialling is available everywhere. To dial the UK from Turkey, dial 0044 then the number (omitting the first zero of the area code).

The tones you hear differ slightly from those heard on British phones, a repeated long tone means that the number is ringing, while alternating shorter tones indicate an engaged number.

USEFUL WORDS AND PHRASES

call	telefon konuşması	*telefon konoosh-massuh*
to call	telefon etmek	*telefon etmek*
code	kod numarası	*kod noomarassuh*
to dial	çevirmek	*cheveer-mek*
dialling tone	çevir sesi	*cheveer sessee*
email address	e-posta adresi	*e-possta adresee*
emergency	imdat	*eemdat*
engaged	meşgul	*mesh-gool*
enquiries	danışma servisi	*danushma serveessee*
extension	dahili	*daheelee*
international call	uluslararası konuşma	*ooloos-lar-arassuh konoosh-massuh*

87

medium token	orta jeton	*orta jeton*
mobile phone	cep telefonu	*jep telefonoo*
number	numara	*noomara*
operator	santral memuru	*santral memooroo*
payphone	umumi telefon	*oomoomee telefon*
phonecard	telefon kartı	*telefon kartuh*
push-button phone	tuşlu telefon	*tooshloo telefon*
reverse charge call	ödemeli konuşma	*urdemelee konooshma*
ringing tone	telefon çalıyor tonu	*telefon chaluh-yor tonoo*
small token	küçük jeton	*kew-chewk jeton*
telephone	telefon	*telefon*
telephone box	telefon kulübesi	*telefon koolew-bessee*
telephone directory	telefon rehberi	*telefon rehberee*
token	jeton	*jeton*
Web site	web sitesi	*web seetesee*
wrong number	yanlış numara	*yanluhsh noomara*

Where is the nearest phone box?
En yakın telefon kulübesi nerede?
en yakuhn telefon koolew-bessee neh-reh-deh

Can I have one/three token(s) for …?
… için bir/üç jeton verir misiniz?
… eecheen beer/ewch jeton vereer meesseeneez

I would like the directory for …
… telefon rehberini rica ediyorum
… telefon rehbereenee reeja edeeyoroom

How much is a call to …?
…-ya telefon ücreti ne kadardır?
…-ya telefon ewj-retee neh kadar-duhr

I would like to reverse the charges
Ödemeli konuşmak istiyorum
urdemelee konooshmak eesteeyoroom

I would like a number in ...
...-de bir numarayı arıyorum
...-de beer noomara-yuh aruh-yoroom

How do I get an outside line?
Nasıl dış hat alabilirim?
nasuhl duhsh hat ala-beeleereem

Hello, this is ... speaking
Alo, ben ...
alo, ben ...

Is that ...?
... ile mi görüşüyorum?
... eeleh mee gurewshew-yoroom

Speaking
Benim
beneem

I would like to speak to ...
... ile görüşmek istiyorum
... eeleh gurewsh-mek eesteeyoroom

Extension ..., please
Dahili ... i istiyorum
daheelee ... ee eesteeyoroom

Please tell him ... called
Lütfen, kendisine ... aradı deyin
lewtfen, kendeesseeneh ... araduh day-yeen

Ask him to call me back, please
Lütfen beni aramasını söyleyin
lewtfen benee aramassuhnuh surlay-yeen

My number is …
Benim numaram …
beneem noomaram …

Do you know where he is?
Nerede olduğunu biliyor musunuz?
neh-reh-deh oldoo-oonoo beeleeyor moo-soonooz

When will he be back?
Ne zaman dönecek?
neh zaman durnejek

Could I leave him a message?
Bir mesaj bırakabilir miyim?
beer messaj buhrakabeleer mee-yeem

I'll ring back later
Sonra tekrar ararım
sonra tekrar araruhm

Sorry, wrong number
Affedersiniz, yanlış numara
af-federseeneez, yanluhsh noomara

What is your fax number/email address?
faks/e-posta adresiniz nedir?
faks/e-possta adreseeneez nedeer

Can I send a fax/email from here?
Buradan faks/e-posta gönderebilir miyim?
booradan faks/e-possta gurn-derebeeleer meeyeem

Did you get my fax/email?
Faksımı/e postamı aldınız mı?
faks-uhmuh/e-posstamuh alduhn<u>uh</u>z muh

Can I use the photocopier/fax machine?
Fotokopi/faks makinesını kullanabilir miyim?
fotokopee/faks makeeneeseen<u>ee</u> kool-lanabeel<u>ee</u>r meey<u>ee</u>m

---

THINGS YOU'LL HEAR

Benim
Speaking

Kendisi şimdi burada yoklar
Sorry, he is not in

Kiminle görüşuyorum?
Who's speaking?

Numaranız kaç?
What's your number?

Sizi arasın mı?
Can he call you back?

Kiminle görüşmek istiyorsunuz?
Whom do you want to speak to?

Yanlış numara çevirdiniz
You've got the wrong number

Saat ...-de dönecek
He'll be back at ...

THINGS YOU'LL SEE

acele/acil	urgent
ahize	receiver, handset
arıza servisi	faults service
atmak	insert
beklemek	wait
bozuk	out of order
bozuk para	coins
cep telefonu	mobile phone
çevirmek	dial
çevir tonu	dialling tone
dahili	extension
faks makinası	fax machine
fotokopi makinası	photocopier
internet	internet
itfaiye	fire brigade
jeton	telephone token(s)
kadran	dial
kaldırın	lift (the receiver)
kısa konuşun!	be brief!
mandal	hook
meslekler rehberi	Yellow Pages
meşgul	engaged
uluslararası	international
santral memuru	operator
tarife	charges
telefon kodu	dialling code
telefon konuşması	call, conversation
telefon numarası	number
telefon rehberi	telephone directory
telesekreter	answering machine
yangın	fire
yerel konuşma	local call
yıldırım	very urgent
yurtdışı	abroad

HEALTH

You are advised to take out full medical insurance to cover the costs of possible treatment in Turkey. There are several foreign hospitals in Istanbul, and many doctors in Turkish hospitals speak a foreign language.

Chemists operate on a rota system which ensures that there is always one chemist open in a town or district at all times. All chemists display a board showing where this duty chemist is located. Turkish chemists are qualified to treat minor injuries.

Useful Words and Phrases

accident	kaza	*kaza*
AIDS	Aids	*eydz*
ambulance	ambülans,	*ambewlanss,*
	cankurtaran	*jankoortaran*
anaemia	kansızlık,	*kanssuhz-luhk,*
	anemi	*anemee*
antibiotic	antibiyotik	*antee-beeyoteek*
appendicitis	apandisit	*apandeesseet*
appendix	kör bağırsak	*kur ba-uhrssak*
aspirin	aspirin	*aspeereen*
asthma	astım	*astuhm*
backache	sırt ağrısı	*surt a-ruhssuh*
bandage	sargı	*sarguh*
bite	sokma	*sokma*
(*mosquito, dog*)	ısırma	*uh-suhrma*
bladder	mesane	*messaneh*
to bleed	kanamak	*kanamak*
blister	kabarcık	*kabarjuhk*
blood	kan	*kan*
blood donor	kan verici	*kan vereejee*
burn	yanık	*yanuhk*
cancer	kanser	*kanser*
chemist	eczacı	*ezzajuh*
chickenpox	suçiçeği	*soocheecheh-ee*

93

cold	soğuk algınlığı	so-ook alguhnluh-uh
concussion	beyin sarsıntısı	beh-yeen sarssuhn-tuhssuh
constipation	kabızlık	kabuhzluhk
corn	nasır	nasuhr
cough	öksürük	urksew-rewk
cut	kesik	kesseek
dentist	dişçi	deesh-chee
diabetes	şeker hastalığı	sheker hastaluh-uh
diarrhoea	ishal	eeshal
dizzy	baş dönmesi	bash durn-messee
doctor	doktor	doktor
earache	kulak ağrısı	koolak a-ruhssuh
fever	ateş	atesh
filling	dolgu	dolgoo
first aid	ilk yardım	eelk yarduhm
flu	grip	greep
fracture	kırık	kuhruhk
German measles	kızamıkçık	kuhzamuhk-chuhk
glasses	gözlük	gurzlewk
haemorrhage	kanama	kanama
hay fever	saman nezlesi	saman nezlessee
headache	baş ağrısı	bash a-ruhssuh
heart attack	kalp krizi	kalp kreezee
hepatitis	hepatit	hepateet
hip	kalça	kalcha
HIV positive	HIV positif	HIV poseeteev
hospital	hastane	hastaneh
ill	hasta	hasta
indigestion	hazımsızlık	hazuhm-suhzluhk
inflammation	iltihap	eelteehap
injection	enjeksiyon, iğne	enjeksseeyon, ee-neh
injury	yaralanma	yaralanma
to itch	kaşınmak	kashuhn-mak
jaw	çene	cheneh

kidney	böbrek	*burbrek*
lump	yumru	*yoomroo*
lung	akciğer	*akjee-er*
measles	kızamık	*kuhzamuhk*
migraine	migren	*meegren*
mumps	kabakulak	*kabakoolak*
nausea	mide bulantısı	*meedeh boolantuhssuh*
neck	boyun	*boyoon*
nurse	hasta bakıcı	*hasta bakuhjuh*
ointment	merhem	*merhem*
operation	ameliyat	*amelee-yat*
optician	göz doktoru	*gurz doktoroo*
pain	ağrı	*a-ruh*
painkiller	ağrı kesici	*a-ruh keseejee*
penicillin	penisilin	*penesseeleen*
pharmacy	eczane	*ezzaneh*
pill	hap	*hap*
plaster (*sticky*)	plaster	*plaster*
plaster of Paris	alçı	*alchuh*
pneumonia	zatürree	*zatewr-reh*
pregnant	hamile,	*hameeleh,*
	gebe	*ghe-beh*
prescription	reçete	*recheteh*
rash	isilik	*eesseeleek*
rheumatism	romatizma	*romateezma*
scald	yanık	*yanuhk*
scratch	bere	*bereh*
sling	askı	*asskuh*
smallpox	çiçek hastalığı	*cheechek hastaluh-uh*
sore	ağrı	*a-ruh*
sore throat	boğaz ağrısı	*bo-az a-ruhssuh*
splinter	çatlama	*chatlama*
sprain	burkulma	*boorkoolma*
sting	yanma	*yanma*
stomach	mide	*meedeh*

95

temperature	ateş	*atesh*
tonsils	bademcik	*bademjik*
tooth	diş	*deesh*
toothache	diş ağrısı	*deesh a-ruhssuh*
travel sickness	yol tutması	*yol tootmassuh*
ulcer	ülser	*ewlsser*
vaccination	aşı	*ashuh*
to vomit	kusmak	*koossmak*
whooping cough	boğmaca	*bo-maja*
wound	yara	*yara*

I have a pain in …
…-de bir ağrı var
…-deh beer a-ruh var

I do not feel well
Kendimi iyi hissetmiyorum
kendeemee ee-yee heess-setmeeyoroom

I feel faint
Halsizlik duyuyorum
halseezleek doo-yoo-yoroom

I feel sick
Midem bulanıyor
meedem boolanuhyor

I feel dizzy
Başım dönüyor
bashuhm durnew-yor

It hurts here
Burası acıyor
boorassuh ajuhyor

It's a sharp pain
Bıçak gibi bir ağrı
buhchak gheebee beer a-ruh

It's a dull pain
Devamlı bir sızı
devamluh beer suhzuh

It hurts all the time
Sürekli ağrıyor
sewreklee a-ruhyor

It only hurts now and then
Arada sırada ağrıyor
arada suhrada a-ruhyor

It hurts when you touch it
Dokunduğunuz zaman acıyor
dokoondoo-oonooz zaman ajuhyor

It hurts more at night
Geceleri daha fazla ağrıyor
ghejeleree daha fazla a-ruhyor

It stings/It aches
Yanıyor/Sızlıyor
yanuhyor/suhzluhyor

I have a temperature
Ateşim var
atesheem var

I'm ... months pregnant
... aylık hamileyim
... 'eye'luhk hameeleh-yeem

I need a prescription for ...
... için bir reçete istiyorum
... *eecheen beer recheteh eesteeyoroom*

I normally take ...
Normal olarak ... alıyorum
normal olarak ... aluhyoroom

Can you take these if you are pregnant/breastfeeding?
Hamileler/bebek emzirenler bunları alabilir mi?
hameelehler/behbek emzeerenler bunlaruh alahbeeleer mee

I'm allergic to ...
...-e allerjim var
...-eh allerjeem var

Have you got anything for ...?
... için bir şey var mı?
... eecheen beer shay var muh

Do I need a prescription for ...?
... için reçete lazım mı?
... eecheen recheteh la-zuhm muh

I've lost a filling
Dolgu düştü
dolgoo dewsh-tew

Things You'll Hear

Günde üç defa ikişer tablet alınız
Take two tablets three times a day

Suyla/Çiğnemek için
With water/For chewing

Günde bir/iki/üç defa
Once/twice/three times a day

Yalnız yatacağınız zaman
Only when you go to bed

Sabahları kahvaltıdan önce
First thing in the morning

Normal olarak hangi ilaçları alıyorsunuz?
What medicines do you usually take?

Bence bir doktora görünmeniz gerekiyor
I think you should see a doctor

Maalesef ondan bizde yok
I'm sorry, we don't have that

O ilaç için doktordan reçete almanız lazım
For that you need a prescription

Onu burada bulamazsınız
You can't get that here

Geçmiş olsun!
Get well!

THINGS YOU'LL SEE

acil vaka	emergency
bekleme salonu	waiting room
cankurtaran	ambulance
çocuk doktoru	paediatrician
dispanser	out-patients' clinic
dişçi	dentist
doktor	doctor
göz doktoru	optician
hastalık sigortası	health insurance
hastane	hospital
hekim	doctor
ilk yardım	first aid
jinekolog	gynaecologist
kulak, burun ve boğaz	ear, nose and throat
muayene	examination
muayenehane	surgery
mütehassıs	specialist
nöbetçi eczane/doktor	duty chemist/doctor
ortopedi uzmanı	orthopaedist
özel bakım ünitesi	intensive care unit
özel hasta	private patient
poliklinik	out-patients' clinic
randevu	appointment
reçete	prescription
reçete ile satılır	prescription only
reçete yazmak	to prescribe
tedavi	treatment
uzman	specialist

CONVERSION TABLES

DISTANCES

Distances are marked in kilometres. To convert kilometres to miles, divide the km by 8 and multiply by 5 (one km being five-eighths of a mile). Convert miles to km by dividing the miles by 5 and multiplying by 8. A mile is 1609 m (1.609 km).

km	miles *or* km	miles
1.61	1	0.62
3.22	2	1.24
4.83	3	1.86
6.44	4	2.48
8.05	5	3.11
9.66	6	3.73
11.27	7	4.35
12.88	8	4.97
14.49	9	5.59
16.10	10	6.21

Other units of length:

1 centimetre	= 0.39 in	1 inch	= 25.4 millimetres
1 metre	= 39.37 in	1 foot	= 0.30 metre (30 cm)
10 metres	= 32.81 ft	1 yard	= 0.91 metre

WEIGHTS

The unit you will come into most contact with is the kilogram (kilo), equivalent to 2 lb 3 oz. To convert kg to lbs, multiply by 2 and add one-tenth of the result (thus, 6 kg x 2 = 12 + 1.2, or 13.2 lbs). One ounce is about 28 grams, and 1 lb is 454 g.

CONVERSION TABLES

grams	ounces	ounces	grams
50	1.76	1	28.3
100	3.53	2	56.7
250	8.81	4	113.4
500	17.63	8	226.8

kg	lbs or kg	lbs
0.45	1	2.20
0.91	2	4.41
1.36	3	6.61
1.81	4	8.82
2.27	5	11.02
2.72	6	13.23
3.17	7	15.43
3.63	8	17.64
4.08	9	19.84
4.53	10	22.04

TEMPERATURE

To convert centigrade or Celsius degrees into Fahrenheit, the accurate method is to multiply the °C figure by 1.8 and add 32. Similarly, to convert °F to °C, subtract 32 from the °F figure and divide by 1.8. This will give you a truly accurate conversion, but takes a little time in mental arithmetic! See the table below.

°C	°F	°C	°F	
-10	14	25	77	
0	32	30	86	
5	41	36.9	98.4	*body temperature*
10	50	40	104	
20	68	100	212	*boiling point*

LIQUIDS

Motorists from the UK will be used to seeing petrol priced per litre (and may even know that one litre is about 1.75 pints). One 'imperial' gallon is roughly 4.5 litres, but American drivers must remember that the US gallon is 3.8 litres (1 litre = 1.06 US quart). In the following table, imperial gallons are used:

litres	gals or l	gals
4.54	1	0.22
9.10	2	0.44
13.64	3	0.66
18.18	4	0.88
22.73	5	1.10
27.27	6	1.32
31.82	7	1.54
36.37	8	1.76
40.91	9	1.98
45.46	10	2.20
90.92	20	4.40
136.38	30	6.60
181.84	40	8.80
227.30	50	11.00

TYRE PRESSURES

lb/sq in	15	18	20	22	24
kg/sq cm	1.1	1.3	1.4	1.5	1.7

lb/sq in	26	28	30	33	35
kg/sq cm	1.8	2.0	2.1	2.3	2.5

MINI-DICTIONARY

about: about 16 yaklaşık onaltı
accelerator gaz pedalı
accident kaza
accommodation kalacak yer
ache ağrı
adaptor (*electrical*) adaptör
address adres
adhesive tutkal
admission charge giriş ücreti
Aegean Ege
after sonra
aftershave tıraş losyonu
again gene
against karşı
air conditioning klima
aircraft uçak
air freshener oda spreyi
airline havayolu
airport havalimanı
Albania Arnavutluk
Albanian (*person, adj*) Arnavut
alcohol alkol
all bütün
  all the streets bütün sokaklar
  that's all, thanks
  hepsi bu kadar, teşekkür ederim
almost hemen hemen
alone yalnız
already şimdiden
always hep
ambulance cankurtaran
America Amerika
American (*person*) Amerikalı
  (*adj*) Amerikan
ancient site tarihi yer
and ve
ankle ayak bileği
another (*different*) başka
  (*further*) daha

answering machine telesekreter
antifreeze antifriz
antique antika
antique shop antikacı
antiseptic antiseptik
apartment daire
aperitif aperitif
appetite iştah
apple elma
application form başvuru formu
appointment randevu
apricot kayısı
aqualung balıkadam hava tüpü
arm kol
art sanat
art gallery sanat galerisi
artist sanatçı
as: as soon as possible en kısa zamanda
ashtray kül tablası
Asia Asya
asleep: he's asleep uyuyor
aspirin aspirin
at: at the post office postanede
  at night geceleyin
  at 3 o'clock saat üçte
Athens Atina
attractive cazip
aunt teyze, hala
Australia Avustralya
Australian (*person*) Avustralyalı
Austria Avusturya
automatic otomatik
away: is it far away? uzak mı?
  go away! git!
awful berbat
axe balta
axle aks

baby bebek

baby wipes nemlendirici temizlik
mendili

baby-sitter çocuk bakıcısı

back (not front) arka
(of body) sırt

backgammon tavla

bad kötü

bait yem

bake pişirmek

baker fırıncı

balcony balkon

ball top
(dance) balo

ballpoint pen tükenmez kalem

banana muz

band (musicians) orkestra

bandage sargı

bank banka

banknote banknot

bar bar
bar of chocolate tablet çikolata

barbecue ızgara

barber's berber

basin (sink) lavabo

basket sepet

bath banyo
to have a bath yıkanmak

bathing hat bone

bathroom banyo

battery pil

beach plaj

beans fasulye

beard sakal

beautiful güzel

because çünkü

bed yatak

bed linen yatak çarşafları

bedroom yatak odası

beef sığır eti

beer bira

before önce

beginner acemi

behind arkada

beige bej

Belgium Belçika

bell (church) çan
(door) zil

belly-dancing göbek dansı, oryantal dans

below altında

belt kemer

beside yanında

best en iyi

better daha iyi

between arasında

bicycle bisiklet

big büyük

bikini bikini

bill hesap

bin liner çöp torbası

bird kuş

birthday doğum gunu
happy birthday! doğum gününüz
kutlu olsun!

birthday present doğum günü hediyesi

biscuit bisküvi

bite (verb) ısırmak
(by insect) sokma

bitter acı

black siyah

blackberry böğürtlen

Black Sea Karadeniz

blanket battaniye

bleach (verb: hair) rengini açmak
(noun) çamaşır suyu

blind (cannot see) kör, ama
(on window) istor

blister kabarcık

blood kan

blouse bluz

blue mavi

boat gemi
(smaller) kayık

body vücut

boil kaynatmak
(on body) çıban

bolt (verb) sürgülemek
(noun: on door) sürgü

bone kemik
bonnet (car) kaporta
book (noun) kitap
   (verb) yer ayırtmak
booking office bilet gişesi
bookshop kitapçı
boot (car) bagaj
   (footwear) çizme
border sınır
boring sıkıcı
born: I was born in … …-de doğdum
Bosphorus İstanbul Boğazı
both her ikisi
   both of them her ikisi de
   both of us her ikimiz de
   both … and … hem … hem de …
bottle şişe
bottle opener şişe açacağı
bottom alt
   (of sea) dip
bowl kase
box kutu
boy oğlan
boyfriend erkek arkadaş
bra sütyen
bracelet bilezik
braces pantolon askısı
brake (noun) fren
   (verb) fren yapmak
brandy konyak
bread ekmek
breakdown (car) arıza
   (nervous) sinir krizi
breakfast kahvaltı
breathe nefes almak
   I can't breathe nefes alamıyorum
bridge köprü
briefcase evrak çantası
British İngiliz
brochure broşür
broken kırık
   (out of order) bozuk
broken leg kırık bacak
brooch broş

brother erkek kardeş
brown kahverengi
bruise çürük
brush (noun) fırça
   (verb) fırçalamak
bucket kova
building bina
Bulgaria Bulgaristan
Bulgarian (person) Bulgar
bumper tampon
burglar hırsız
burn (verb) yanmak
   (noun) yanık
bus otobüs
bus station otobüs terminali
business iş
   it is none of your business
   seni ilgilendirmez
busy (person, telephone) meşgul
   (crowded) kalabalık
but ama
butcher kasap
butter tereyağı
button düğme
buy satın almak
by: by the window pencerenin yanında
   by Friday Cumaya kadar
   by myself tek başıma
Byzantine Bizans

cabbage lahana
cable car teleferik
cake pasta
calculator hesap makinesi
call: what's this called? bunun adı
   nedir?
camel deve
camera fotoğraf makinesi
campsite kamping
camshaft kam mili
can (tin) teneke kutu
can: can you come? gelebilir misiniz?
Canada Kanada

Canadian *(person)* Kanadalı
cancer kanser
candle mum
canoe kano
cap *(bottle)* kapak
  (hat) kasket
car otomobil
car seat *(for a baby)* çocuk koltuğu
caravan karavan
carburettor karbüratör
card kart
cardigan hırka
careful dikkatlı
  be careful! dikkat et!
carpet halı
carriage *(train)* vagon
carrot havuç
case valiz
cash nakit para
  (coins) bozuk para
  to pay cash nakit ödemek
cassette kaset
cassette player kasetli teyp
castle kale
cat kedi
cauliflower karnabahar
cave mağara
cemetery mezarlık
centre merkez
certificate belge
chair iskemle
chambermaid oda hizmetçisi
change *(noun: money)* bozuk para
  (verb: clothes) üstünü değiştirmek
cheap ucuz
cheers! şerefe
cheese peynir
chemist *(shop)* eczane
cheque çek
chequebook çek defteri
cherry kiraz
chess satranç
chest göğüs
chewing gum çiklet

chicken tavuk
child çocuk
children çocuklar
china porselen
China Çin
Chinese *(person)* Çinli
chips patates kızartması
chocolate çikolata
  box of chocolates bir kutu çikolata
chop *(food)* pirzola
  (to cut) doğramak
Christian Hıristiyan
church kilise
cigar puro
cigarette sigara
cinema sinema
city şehir
city centre şehir merkezi
class sınıf
classical music klasik müzik
clean temiz
clear *(obvious)* açık
  (water) duru
  is that clear? anlaşıldı mı?
clever akıllı
clock saat
  (alarm) çalar saat
close *(near)* yakın
  (stuffy) havasız
  (verb) kapatmak
  the shop is closed dükkan kapalı
clothes giyim eşyası
club kulüp
  (cards) sinek
coach yolcu otobüsü
  (of train) yolcu vagonu
coach station otogar
coat palto
coat hanger askı
cockroach hamamböceği
coffee kahve
coin madeni para
cold *(illness)* soğuk algınlığı
  (adj) soğuk

collar yaka
collection *(stamps etc)* koleksiyon
colour renk
colour film renkli film
comb *(noun)* tarak
  (verb) taramak
come gelmek
  I come from … …-den geliyorum
  we came last week geçen hafta geldik
  come here! buraya gel!
communication cord imdat freni
compartment kompartıman
complicated karmaşık
concert konser
conditioner *(hair)* balsam
conductor *(bus)* biletçi
  (orchestra) şef
congratulations! tebrikler!
constipation kabızlık
consulate konsolosluk
contact lenses kontak lensler
contraceptive gebeliği önleyici
cook *(noun)* aşçı
  (verb) pişirmek
cooking utensils kap kacak
cool serin
copper bakır
cork mantar
corkscrew tirbuşon
corner köşe
corridor koridor
cosmetics makyaj malzemesi
cost *(noun)* fiyat
  what does it cost? fiyatı ne kadar?
cotton wool idrofil pamuk
cough *(verb)* öksürmek
  (noun) öksürük
country *(state)* ülke
  (not town) kır
cousin *(male)* kuzen
  (female) kuzin
crab pavurya
cramp kramp
crayfish kerevit

cream *(for cake etc)* krema
  (lotion) krem
credit card kredi kartı
Crete Girit
crew mürettebat
crisps çips
crowded kalabalık
cruise deniz gezisi
crutches koltuk değnekleri
cry *(weep)* ağlamak
  (shout) bağırmak
cucumber salatalık
cuff links kol düğmesi
cup fincan
cupboard dolap
curls bukle
curtain perde
customs Gümrük
cut *(noun)* kesik
  (verb) kesmek
Cyprus Kıbrıs

dad baba
dairy *(shop)* sütçü dükkanı
damp nemli
dance dans
dangerous tehlikeli
Dardanelles Çanakkale Boğazı
dark karanlık
  (colour) koyu
daughter kız
day gün
dead ölü
deaf sağır
dear *(person)* değerli
  (expensive) pahalı
deck chair şezlong
deep derin
deliberately kasten
dentist dişçi
dentures protez
deny inkar etmek
  I deny it reddediyorum

deodorant deodoran

department store büyük mağaza

departure kalkış

develop (a film) banyo edip basmak

diamond (jewel) elmas

   (cards) karo

diarrhoea ishal

diary günce

dictionary sözlük

die ölmek

diesel dizel

different başka

  that's different o başka

  I'd like a different one bir başkasını

  istiyorum

difficult zor

dining room yemek salonu

dinner akşam yemeği

dirty kirli

disabled sakat

disposible nappies kağıt bebek bezi

distributor (in car) distribütör

dive dalmak

diving board tramplen

divorced boşanmış

do yapmak

doctor doktor

document belge

dog köpek

doll bebek

dollar dolar

door kapı

down aşağı

drawing pin raptiye

dress elbise

drink (verb) içmek

  (soft drink) içecek

  (alcoholic) içki

  would you like a drink? bir şey

  içmek ister misiniz?

drinking water içme suyu

drive (verb) sürmek

driver şoför

driving licence şoför ehliyeti

drunk sarhoş

dry kuru

dry cleaner kuru temizleyici

dummy (for baby) emzik

during sırasında

dustbin çöp tenekesi

duster toz bezi

duty-free gümrüksüz

each tanesi

  fifty thousand lira each tanesi

  elli bin lira

early erken

earring küpe

ears kulaklar

east doğu

easy kolay

egg yumurta

either: either of them ikisinden biri

  either ... or ... ya ... ya ...

elastic elastiki

elastic band lastik bant

elbow dirsek

electric elektrikli

electricity elektrik

else: something else bir başka bir şey

  someone else başka birisi

  somewhere else başka bir yerde

email e-posta

email address e-posta adresi

embarrassing utandırıcı

embassy elçilik

emerald zümrüt

emergency acil durum

empty boş

end son

engaged (couple) nişanlı

  (occupied) meşgul

engine (motor) motor

England İngiltere

English İngiliz

  (language) İngilizce

Englishman İngiliz

Englishwoman İngiliz kadını
enlargement büyültme
enough yeter
entertainment eğlence
entrance giriş
envelope zarf
escalator yürüyen merdiven
especially özellikle
Europe Avrupa
evening akşam
every her
everyone herkes
everything her şey
everywhere her yerde
example örnek
  for example örneğin
excellent mükemmel
excess baggage fazla bagaj
exchange (*verb*) değiştirmek
exchange rate döviz kuru
excursion gezinti
excuse me! affedersiniz!
exit çıkış
expensive pahalı
explain açıklamak
extension lead uzatma kablosu
eye(s) göz(ler)
eye drops göz damlası

face yüz
faint (*unclear*) belirsiz
  (*verb*) bayılmak
  to feel faint halsizlik duymak
fair (*funfair*) panayır
  (*just*) haklı
  it's not fair bu haksızlık
false teeth takma dişler
family aile
fan (*ventilator*) vantilatör
  (*enthusiast*) hayran
fan belt vantilatör kayışı
far uzak
  how far is …? … ne kadar uzaktadır?

fare taşıma ücreti
farm çiftlik
farmer çiftçi
fashion moda
fast hızlı
fat (*adj*) şişman
  (*on meat etc*) yağ
father baba
fax machine faks makinası
feel (*touch*) dokunmak
  I feel hot çok sıcak
  I feel like … … istiyorum
  I don't feel well kendimi iyi hissetmiyorum
feet ayaklar
felt-tip pen keçe uçlu kalem
ferry feribot, araba vapuru
fever ateş
fiancé(e) nişanlı
field tarla
fig incir
filling (*tooth*) dolgu
  (*sandwich etc*) iç
film film
filter filtre
finger parmak
fire ateş
  (*blaze*) yangın
fire extinguisher yangın söndürme aleti
firework havai fişek
first birinci
first aid ilk yardım
first floor birinci kat
first name öz ad
fish balık
fishing balık tutmak
  to go fishing balık avına çıkmak
fishing rod olta kamışı
fishmonger balıkçı
fizzy gazlı
flag bayrak
flash (*camera*) flaş
flat (*level*) düz
  (*apartment*) daire

flavour tat
flea pire
flight uçuş
flip flops tokyo
flippers paletler
flour un
flower çiçek
flu grip
flute flüt
  (reed) ney
fly (verb) uçmak
  (insect) sinek
fog sis
folk dance halk oyunu
folk music halk müziği
food yiyecek
food poisoning gıda zehirlenmesi
foot ayak
football futbol
  (ball) top
for için
  for me benim için
  what for? niçin?
  for a week bir hafta için
foreigner yabancı
forest orman
fork çatal
fortnight iki hafta
fountain çeşme
fourth dördüncü
fracture kırık
France Fransa
free serbest
  (no cost) bedava
freezer buzluk
French (language) Fransızca
Frenchman Fransız
Frenchwoman Fransız kadını
fridge buzdolabı
friend arkadaş
friendly dost
from: from ... to ... ...-den ...-e
front: in front of ... ... -in önünde
frost don

fruit meyva
fruit juice meyva suyu
fry kızartmak
frying pan tava
full dolu
  I'm full doydum
  full board tam pansiyon
funnel (for pouring) huni
funny komik
  (odd) acayip
furniture mobilya

garage garaj
  (petrol station) benzin istasyonu
garden bahçe
gear vites
gear lever vites kolu
German (person) Alman
Germany Almanya
get (fetch) getirmek
  have you got ...? ... var mı?
  to get the train trene binmek
get back: we get back tomorrow
  yarın dönüyoruz
  to get something back bir şeyi geri
  almak
get in girmek
  (arrive) varmak
get out çıkmak
get up (rise) kalkmak
gift hediye
gin cin
girl kız
girlfriend kız arkadaş
give vermek
glad memnun
  I'm glad memnunum
glass cam
  (to drink) bardak
glasses gözlük
gloss prints parlak tab
gloves eldiven
glue zamk

go gitmek
  I'm going to Istanbul
  İstanbul'a gidiyorum
goggles koruyucu gözlük
gold altın
good iyi
goodbye hoşça kal
government hükûmet
granddaughter kız torun
grandfather büyükbaba
grandmother büyükanne
grandson erkek torun
grapes üzüm
grass ot
Great Britain Büyük Britanya
Greece Yunanistan
Greek (*person*) Yunanlı
  (*ethnic Greek*) Rum
  (*language*) Rumca
Greek Orthodox Rum Ortodoks Kilisesi
green yeşil
grey gri
grill ızgara
grocer (*shop*) bakkal
ground floor zemin kat
groundsheet su geçirmez yaygı
guarantee (*noun*) garanti
  (*verb*) garanti etmek
guard muhafız
  (*train*) kondüktör
guide book rehber
guitar gitar
gun (*rifle*) tüfek
  (*pistol*) tabanca

hair saç
haircut (*for man*) saç tıraşı
  (*for woman*) saç kesme
hairdresser kuaför
hairdryer saç kurutma makinası
half yarım
  half an hour yarım saat
half board yarım pansiyon

ham jambon
hamburger hamburger
hammer çekiç
hand el
handbag el çantası
handbrake el freni
handkerchief mendil
handle (*door*) kapı tokmağı
handsome yakışıklı
hangover içki sersemliği
happy mutlu
harbour liman
hard sert
  (*difficult*) zor
hat şapka
have: I don't have … … im yok
  I don't have a ticket biletim yok
  can I have …? … istiyorum
  do you have …? … var mı?
  I have to go now şimdi gitmem lazım
hay fever saman nezlesi
he o
head baş
headache baş ağrısı
headlights farlar
headscarf başörtüsü
hear duymak
hearing aid işitme cihazı
heart kalp
heart attack kalp krizi
heating ısıtma
heavy ağır
heel topuk
hello merhaba
help (*noun*) yardım
  (*verb*) yardım etmek
  help! imdat!
hepatitis hepatit
her o
  it's for her onun için
  give it to her ona ver
  her house/her shoes
  onun evi/onun ayakkabıları
  this is hers bu onun

high yüksek

highway code trafik kurallari

hill tepe

him o
  it's for him onun için
  give it to him ona ver

hire kiralamak

his: his book/his shoes
  onun kitabı/onun ayakkabıları
  this is his bu onun

history tarih

hitchhike otostop yapmak

HIV positive HIV positif

hobby merak

holiday tatil, bayram

Holland Hollanda

homosexual homoseksüel

honest dürüst

honey bal

honeymoon balayı

hookah nargile

horn (car) klakson
  (animal) boynuz

horrible korkunç

hospitable konuksever

hospital hastane

hot sıcak
  (spicy) acı

hour saat

house ev

how? nasıl?

hungry: I'm hungry acıktım

hurry: I'm in a hurry acelem var

husband koca

I ben

ice buz

ice cream dondurma

ice cube parça buz

if eğer

ignition ateşleme

ill hasta

immediately hemen

impossible imkansız

in -da, -de
  in Istanbul İstanbul'da
  in my room odamda
  in English İngilizcede

India Hindistan

Indian (person) Hintli
  (adj) Hint

indicator gösterge

indigestion hazımsızlık

infection enfeksiyon

information bilgi
  (travel) danışma

injection enjeksiyon

injury yaralanma

ink mürekkep

inner tube iç lastik

insect böcek

insect repellent böcek ilacı

insomnia uykusuzluk

insurance sigorta

interesting ilginç

internet internet

interpret tercüme etmek

invitation davet

Iran İran

Iraq Irak

Ireland İrlanda

Irishman İrlandalı

Irishwoman İrlandalı kadın

iron (metal) demir
  (for clothes) ütü

ironmonger nalbur

Islam İslam

Islamic İslami

island ada

it o

Italy İtalya

itch (noun) kaşıntı
  it itches kaşınıyor

jacket ceket

jam reçel

113

jazz caz
jealous kıskanç
  he is jealous kıskanıyor
jeans blucin
jellyfish denizanası
jeweller kuyumcu
job iş
jog (verb) koşmak
  to go for a jog koşuya çıkmak
joke şaka
journey seyahat
jumper kazak
just: it's just arrived şimdi geldi
  I've just one left
  yalnız bir tane kaldı

kebab kebap
key anahtar
kidney böbrek
kilo kilo
kilometre kilometre
kiss (noun) öpücük
kitchen mutfak
knee diz
knife bıçak
knit örmek
know: I don't know bilmiyorum
Koran Kur'an

label etiket
lace dantel
laces (of shoe) ayakkabı bağları
lady hanım, bayan
lake göl
lamb kuzu
lamp lamba
lampshade abajur
land (not sea) kara
  (verb: aeroplane) inmek
  (from boat) karaya çıkmak
language dil
large büyük
114

last (final) son
  last week geçen hafta
  last month geçen ay
  at last! en sonunda!
late: it's getting late geç oldu
  the bus is late
  otobüs geç kaldı
laugh gülmek
launderette otomatlı çamaşırhane
laundry (place) çamaşırhane
  (dirty clothes) kirli çamaşır
laxative müshil
lazy tembel
leaf yaprak
leaflet broşür
learn öğrenmek
leather deri
leave (go away) ayrılmak
  (object) bırakmak
left (not right) sol
  nothing left hiç bir şey kalmadı
left luggage emanet
leg bacak
lemon limon
lemonade limonata
  (fizzy) gazoz
length uzunluk
lens mercek
less daha az
lesson ders
letter mektup
letter box mektup kutusu
lettuce marul
library kütüphane
licence izin belgesi
life hayat
lift (in building) asansör
  could you give me a lift? beni de
  alabilir misiniz?
light (not heavy) hafif
  (not dark) aydınlık
light meter pozometre
lighter çakmak
lighter fuel çakmak benzini

like: **I like you** senden hoşlanıyorum
  I like swimming yüzmeyi seviyorum
  it's like ... ... gibi
lime *(fruit)* misket limonu
lip salve dudak merhemi
lipstick ruj
liqueur likör
lira lira
list liste
litre litre
litter çöp
little *(small)* küçük
  it's a little big biraz büyük
  just a little azıcık
liver karaciğer
lobster ıstakoz
long uzun
  how long does it take? ne kadar sürer?
lorry kamyon
lost property kayıp eşya
lot: a lot çok
loud yüksek sesle
  (colour) çiğ
lounge salon
love *(noun)* sevgi
  (verb) sevmek
lover sevgili
low alçak
luck şans
luggage bagaj
luggage rack bagaj rafı
lunch öğle yemeği

magazine dergi
mail posta
make yapmak
make-up makyaj
man adam
manager yönetici
map harita
  a map of Istanbul İstanbul şehir
  planı
marble mermer

margarine margarin
market çarşı
marmalade portakal reçeli
married evli
mascara rimel
mast direk
match *(light)* kibrit
  (sport) maç
material *(cloth)* kumaş
mattress şilte
maybe belki
me: it's me benim
  it's for me benim için
  give it to me bana ver
meal yemek
meat et
mechanic makina tamircisi
medicine ilaç
  (science) tıp
Mediterranean *(noun)* Akdeniz
meeting toplantı
melon kavun
men's toilet erkeler tuvaleti
menu yemek listesi
message mesaj
midday öğle
middle: in the middle ortada
midnight gece yarısı
milk süt
minaret minare
mine: this is mine bu benim
mineral water maden suyu
minute dakika
mirror ayna
mistake hata
  to make a mistake hata yapmak
mobile phone cep telefonu
monastery manastır
money para
month ay
monument anıt
moon ay
moped moped
more daha

115

morning sabah
  in the morning sabahleyin
mosaic mozaik
Moslem Müslüman
mosque cami
  Blue Mosque Sultan Ahmet Camisi
mosquito sivrisinek
mother anne
motorbike motosiklet
motorboat motorbot
motorway otoyol
mountain dağ
mouse fare
moustache bıyık
mouth ağız
move hareket etmek
  don't move! kımıldama!
  (house) taşınmak
movie filim
Mr Bay
Mrs Bayan
much: not much fazla değil
  much better çok daha iyi
mug kupa
mule katır
mum anne
museum müze
mushroom mantar
music müzik
musical instrument müzik aleti
musician müzisyen
mussels midye
mustard hardal
my: my bag benim çantam
  my keys benim anahtarlarım
mythology mitoloji

nail (metal) çivi
  (finger) tırnak
nailfile tırnak törpüsü
nail polish tırnak cilası
name ad
nappy çocuk bezi

narrow dar
near: near the door kapının yakınında
  near London Londra yakınında
necessary gerekli
necklace kolye
need (verb) lazım olmak
  I need ... bana ... lazım
  there's no need gerek yok
needle iğne
negative (photo) negatif
neither: neither of them hiçbiri
  neither ... nor ... ne ... ne de ...
nephew yeğen
never asla
new yeni
news haber
newsagent gazete bayii
newspaper gazete
New Zealand Yeni Zelanda
New Zealander Yeni Zelandalı
next bir sonraki
  next week gelecek hafta
  next month gelecek ay
nice hoş
niece yeğen
night gece
nightclub gece kulübü
nightdress gecelik
no (response) hayır
  I have no money param yok
noisy gürültülü
north kuzey
Northern Ireland Kuzey İrlanda
nose burun
not değil
notebook not defteri
nothing hiçbir şey
novel roman
now şimdi
nowhere hiçbir yerde
nude çıplak
number sayı
  (telephone) numara
number plate plaka

nurse hasta bakıcı
nut *(fruit)* fısuk
  (for bolt) somun

occasionally arada sırada
octopus ahtapot
of -in, -ın, -un, -ün
  the name of the village
  köyün adı
office ofis
often sık sık
oil yağ
ointment merhem
OK tamam
old eski
  (of person) yaşlı
olive zeytin
omelette omlet
on -da, -de
  on the beach plajda
  on the terrace terasta
  a book on Turkey
  Türkiye hakkında bir kitap
one bir
onion soğan
only yalnız
open *(verb)* açmak
  (adj) açık
opposite: opposite the hotel
  otelin karşısında
optician gözlükçü
or veya
orange *(colour)* turuncu
  (fruit) portakal
orange juice portakal suyu
orchestra orkestra
ordinary *(normal)* olağan
our bizim
  this is ours bu bizim
out: he's out dışarı çıktı
outside dışarıda
over üzerinde
  over there orada

overtake geçmek
oyster istiridye

pack of cards iskambil destesi
package ambalaj
  (parcel) paket
packet paket
  a packet of … bir paket …
padlock asma kilit
page sayfa
pain ağrı
paint *(noun)* boya
pair çift
Pakistan Pakistan
Pakistani Pakistanlı
pale soluk
pancakes gözleme
paper kağıt
  (newspaper) gazete
paracetamol parasetamol
parcel koli
pardon? efendim?
parents ana baba
park *(noun)* park
  (verb) park etmek
party *(celebration, political)* parti
  (group) grup
passenger yolcu
passport pasaport
pasta makarna
path yol
pavement kaldırım
pay ödemek
peach şeftali
peanuts yerfıstığı
pear armut
pearl inci
peas bezelye
pedestrian yaya
peg *(for clothes)* mandal
pen dolma kalem
pencil kurşun kalem
pencil sharpener kalemtıraş

117

penfriend mektup arkadaşı
peninsula yarımada
penknife çakı
people halk
pepper (& salt) karabiber
  (red/green) biber
peppermints nane şekeri
per: per night geceliği
perfect mükemmel
perfume parfüm
perhaps belki
perm perma
petrol benzin
petrol station benzin istasyonu
petticoat jüpon
phonecard telefon kartı
photocopier fotokopi makinası
photograph (noun) fotoğraf
  (verb) fotoğraf çekmek
photographer fotoğrafçı
phrase book yabancı dil kılavuzu
piano piyano
pickpocket yankesici
picnic piknik
piece parça
pillow yastık
pilot pilot
pin toplu iğne
pine (tree) çam
pineapple ananas
pink pembe
pipe (for smoking) pipo
  (for water) boru
pizza pizza
place yer
plant bitki
plaster (for cut) plaster
plastic plastik
plastic bag naylon torba
plate tabak
platform platform
  (trains) peron
play (theatre) oyun
pleasant hoş
118

please lütfen
plug (electrical) fiş
  (sink) tıkaç
pocket cep
poison zehir
police polis
police officer polis
police station karakol
politics politika
poor yoksul
  (bad quality) kalitesiz
pop music pop müziği
pork domuz eti
port (harbour) liman
porter (for luggage) hamal
  (hotel) kapıcı
possible mümkün
post (noun) posta
  (verb) postalamak
post box posta kutusu
postcard kartpostal
poster afiş
postman postacı
post office postane
potato patates
poultry kümes hayvanları
pound (money) lira
  (weight) libre
powder toz
  (make up) pudra
pram çocuk arabası
prawn karides
  (bigger) büyük karides
prescription reçete
pretty (beautiful) güzel
  (quite) oldukça
priest rahip
private özel
problem sorun
  what's the problem? sorun nedir?
public halka açık
pull çekmek
puncture lastik patlaması
purple mor

purse para çantası
push itmek
pushchair puset
pyjamas pijama

quality kalite
quay rıhtım
question soru
queue *(noun)* kuyruk
  (verb) kuyruğa girmek
quick çabuk
quiet sessiz
quite *(fairly)* oldukça
  (fully) tamamen

radiator radyatör
radio radyo
radish turp
railway line demiryolu hattı
rain yağmur
raincoat yağmurluk
raisins kuru üzüm
rare *(uncommon)* nadir
  (steak) az pişmiş
rat sıçan
razor blade jilet
read okumak
reading lamp masa lambası
  (bed) başucu lambası
ready hazır
rear lights arka sinyal lambaları
receipt makbuz
receptionist resepsiyon memuru
record *(music)* plak
  (sporting etc) rekor
record player pikap
record shop plakçı dükkanı
red kırmızı
refreshments meşrubat
registered letter taahhütlü mektup
relative *(noun)* akraba
relax dinlenmek

religion din
remember hatırlamak
  I don't remember hatırlamıyorum
rent *(verb)* kiralamak
reservation rezervasyon
rest *(remainder)* kalan
  (relaxation) dinlenme
restaurant restoran
restaurant car vagon restoran
return geri dönmek
Rhodes Rodos
rice *(cooked)* pilav
  (uncooked) pirinç
rich zengin
right *(correct)* doğru
  (direction) sağ
ring *(to call)* telefon etmek
  (wedding etc) yüzük
ripe olgun
river nehir
road yol
rock *(stone)* kaya
  (music) rok müziği
roll *(bread)* sandviç ekmeği
  (verb) yuvarlanmak
roller skates patenler
Romania Romanya
Romanian *(person, adj)* Romen
roof dam
  (flat) taraça
room oda
  (space) yer
rope ip
rose gül
round *(circular)* yuvarlak
  it's my round sıra bende
rowing boat kayık
rubber *(eraser)* silgi
  (material) lastik
rubbish çöp
ruby *(stone)* yakut
rucksack sırt çantası
rug *(mat)* kilim
  (blanket) battaniye

119

ruins harabeler
ruler *(for drawing)* cetvel
rum rom
run *(person)* koşmak
runway pist
Russia Rusya
Russian *(person, adj)* Rus

sad üzgün
safe emniyetli
safety emniyet
sailing boat yelkenli
salad salata
salami salam
sale *(at reduced prices)* indirimli satış
salmon som balığı
salt tuz
same: the same … aynı …
  same again, please
  lütfen gene aynısından
samovar semaver
sand kum
sandals sandal
sand dunes kumullar
sandwich sandviç
sanitary towels ped
sauce sos
saucepan tencere
sauna sauna
sausage sosis
say söylemek
  what did you say? ne dedin?
  how do you say …? … nasıl denir?
scarf atkı
  (head) eşarp, başörtüsü
school okul
scissors makas
Scotland İskoçya
Scottish İskoç
screw vida
screwdriver tornavida
sea deniz
seafood deniz ürünleri

seat oturacak yer
seat belt emniyet kemeri
second *(adj)* ikinci
see görmek
  I can't see göremiyorum
  I see anlıyorum
sell satmak
send göndermek
separate ayrı
separated ayrılmış
serious ciddi
serviette peçete
several birkaç
sew dikmek
shampoo şampuan
shave *(noun)* tıraş
  (verb) tıraş olmak
shaving foam tıraş köpüğü
shawl şal
she o
sheet çarşaf
shell *(on beach)* deniz kabuğu
ship gemi
shirt gömlek
shoe ayakkabı
shoelaces ayakkabı bağları
shoe polish ayakkabı cilası
shop dükkan
shopping alışveriş
  to go shopping alışverişe çıkmak
short kısa
shorts şort
shoulder omuz
shower *(bath)* duş
  (rain) sağanak
shrimp karides
shutter *(camera)* obdüratör
  (window) kepenk
sick *(ill)* hasta
  I feel sick midem bulanıyor
side *(edge)* kenar
  I'm on her side
  ben ondan yanayım
sidelights park lambaları

sights: the sights of ... ...-nin görmeye
  değer yerleri
silk ipek
silver (colour) gümüş rengi
  (metal) gümüş
simple basit
sing şarkı söylemek
single (one) tek
  (unmarried) bekar
sister kız kardeş
skid (verb) kaymak
skin cleanser cilt temizleyici
skirt eteklik
sky gök
sleep (noun) uyku
  (verb) uyumak
  to go to sleep uykuya dalmak
sleeping bag uyku tulumu
sleeping pill uyku ilacı
slippers terlikler
slow yavaş
small küçük
smell (noun) koku
  (verb: give off smell) kokmak
  (detect smell) koklamak
smile (noun) gülümseme
  (verb) gülümsemek
smoke (noun) duman
  (verb) sigara içmek
snack hafif yemek
snorkel şnorkel
snow kar
so: so good o kadar iyi
  not so much o kadar değil
soaking solution (for contact lenses)
  koruyucu sıvı
socks çoraplar
soda water maden sodası
somebody birisi
somehow her nasılsa
something bir şey
sometimes bazen
somewhere bir yerde
son oğul

song şarkı
soon kısa zamanda
sorry! pardon!
  I'm sorry özür dilerim
soup çorba
sour ekşi
south güney
South Africa Güney Afrika
South African (person) Güney Afrikalı
souvenir hatıra
spade (shovel) bel
  (cards) maça
Spain İspanya
Spanish (adj) İspanyol
spanner somun anahtarı
spares yedek
spark(ing) plug buji
speak konuşmak
  do you speak ...? ... biliyor musunuz?
  I don't speak ... ... bilmiyorum
speed hız
speed limit hız tahdidi
speedometer kilometre saati
spider örümcek
spinach ıspanak
spoon kaşık
sprain burkulma
spring (mechanical) yay
  (season) ilkbahar
stadium stadyum
staircase merdiven
stairs merdivenler
stamp pul
stapler tel zımba
star yıldız
start başlangıç
  (verb) başlamak
station istasyon
statue heykel
steak biftek
steal çalmak
  it's been stolen çalındı
steering wheel direksiyon
stewardess hostes

sticky tape selobant
sting *(noun)* sokma
  (verb) sokmak
  it stings yanıyor
stockings çoraplar
stomach mide
stomachache karın ağrısı
stop *(verb)* durmak
  (bus stop) durak
  stop! dur!
storm fırtına
strawberry çilek
stream *(small river)* dere
street sokak
string *(cord)* ip
  (guitar etc) tel
student öğrenci
stupid aptal
suburbs banliyö
sugar şeker
suit *(noun)* takım elbise
  (verb) yakışmak
  it suits you sana yakışıyor
suitcase valiz
sun güneş
sunbathe güneşlenmek
sunburn güneş yanığı
sunglasses güneş gözlüğü
sunny: it's sunny hava güneşli
suntan bronz ten
suntan lotion güneş losyonu
supermarket süpermarket
supplement ek
surname soyadı
sweat *(noun)* ter
  (verb) terlemek
sweatshirt svetşört
sweet *(not sour)* tatlı
  (candy) şeker
swimming costume mayo
swimming pool yüzme havuzu
swimming trunks mayo
Swiss *(person)* İsviçreli
switch *(noun)* anahtar

Switzerland İsviçre
synagogue sinagog
Syria Suriye
Syrian *(person, adj)* Suriyeli

table masa
tablet tablet
take almak
takeoff kalkış
take off *(verb)* kalkmak
talcum powder talk pudrası
talk *(noun)* konuşma
  (verb) konuşmak
tall *(person)* uzun boylu
  (thing) yüksek
tampon tampon
tangerine mandalina
tap musluk
tapestry duvar halısı
taxi taksi
tea çay
team takım
tea towel kurulama bezi
telephone *(noun)* telefon
  (verb) telefon etmek
telephone box telefon kulübesi
telephone call telefon konuşması
television televizyon
temperature *(heat)* sıcaklık
  (fever) ateş
temple tapınak
tent çadır
tent peg çadır kazığı
tent pole çadır direği
than: larger than … …-den büyük
thank *(verb)* teşekkür etmek
  thanks teşekkürler
  thank you teşekkür ederim
that: that bus o otobüs
  that man o adam
  that woman o kadın
  what's that? o nedir?
  I think that … sanıyorum ki …

their: their room onların odası
  their books onların kitapları
  this is theirs bu onların
them: it's them onlar
  it's for them onlar için
  give it to them onlara ver
then o zaman
there orada
  there is ... ... var
  there is not ... ... yok
thermal spring kaplıca
these: these things bu şeyler
  these are mine bunlar benim
they onlar
thick kalın
thin ince
thing şey
think düşünmek
  I think so bence öyle
  I'll think about it düşüneyim
third üçüncü
thirsty: I'm thirsty susadım
this: this bus bu otobüs
  this woman bu kadın
  what's this? bu nedir?
  this is Mr ... ... Bay ... -dır
those: those things o şeyler
  those are his onlar onun
throat boğaz
throat pastilles boğaz pastilleri
through içinden
  through the town
  şehrin içinden
thumb başparmak
thunderstorm gök gürültülü fırtına
ticket bilet
tie (noun) kravat
  (verb) bağlamak
tights külotlu çorap
time zaman
  what's the time? saat kaç?
timetable tarife
tin teneke kutu
tin opener konserve açacağı

tip (money) bahşiş
  (end) uç
tired yorgun
  I feel tired yorgunum
tissues kağıt mendil
to: to England İngiltere'ye
  to the station istasyona
  to the doctor doktora
toast tost
tobacco tütün
today bugün
toe ayak parmağı
together birlikte
toilet tuvalet
toilet paper tuvalet kağıdı
tomato domates
tomato juice domates suyu
tomorrow yarın
tongue dil
tonic tonik
tonight bu gece
too (also) de
  (excessively) fazla
tooth diş
toothache diş ağrısı
toothbrush diş fırçası
toothpaste diş macunu
torch el feneri
tour tur
tourist turist
towel havlu
tower kule
town şehir
town hall belediye binası
toy oyuncak
track suit eşofman
tractor traktör
tradition gelenek
traffic trafik
traffic jam trafik tıkanıklığı
traffic lights trafik lambası
trailer römork
train tren
translate tercüme etmek

transmission *(for car)* transmisyon
travel agency seyahat acentesi
traveller's cheque seyahat çeki
tray tepsi
tree ağaç
trousers pantolon
Troy Truva
try denemek
tunnel tünel
Turk *(person)* Türk
Turkey Türkiye
Turkish Türk
   (language) Türkçe
Turkish bath hamam
Turkish coffee Türk kahvesi
Turkish delight lokum
turquoise *(stone)* firuze
tweezers cımbız
typewriter daktilo
tyre lastik

umbrella şemsiye
uncle amca
under altında
underpants külot
university üniversite
unmarried bekar
until kadar
unusual olağandışı
up yukarı
   (upwards) yukarıya
urgent acil
us biz
   it's for us bizim için
   give it to us bize ver
use *(noun)* kullanım
   (verb) kullanmak
   it's no use faydasız
useful faydalı
usual olağan
usually genellikle

vacancy *(room)* boş oda
vacuum flask termos
valley vadi
valve valf
vanilla vanilya
vase vazo
veal dana eti
vegetables sebze
vegetarian *(person)* etyemez
vehicle taşıt
very çok
   very much çok
vest fanila
video tape video kaset
view manzara
viewfinder vizör
villa villa
village köy
vinegar sirke
violin keman
visa vize
visit *(noun)* ziyaret
   (verb) ziyaret etmek
visitor konuk
vitamin tablet vitamin hapı
vodka votka
voice ses

wait beklemek
waiter/waitress garson
   waiter! garson!
waiting room bekleme salonu
Wales Galler Ülkesi
walk *(noun)* yürüyüş
   (verb) yürümek
   to go for a walk yürüyüşe çıkmak
wall duvar
wallet cüzdan
war savaş
wardrobe gardırop
warm sıcak
washing powder deterjan
washing-up liquid bulaşık deterjanı

wasp yabanarısı
watch (noun) saat
  (verb) seyretmek
water su
waterfall çağlayan
waterpipe (to smoke) nargile
wave (noun) dalga
  (verb) sallamak
we biz
weather hava
Web site web sitesi
wedding düğün
week hafta
wellingtons lastik çizme
Welsh Gal'li
west batı
wet ıslak
what? ne?
wheel tekerlek
wheelchair tekerlekli sandalye
when? ne zaman?
where? nerede?
which? hangi?
whisky viski
white beyaz
who? kim?
why? neden?
wide geniş
wife hanım
wind rüzgar
window pencere
windscreen ön cam
wine şarap
wine list şarap listesi
wing kanat
with ile
  with sugar şekerli
without -siz
  without sugar şekersiz
woman kadın
women's toilet bayanlar tuvaleti
wood (forest) orman
  (material) tahta
wool yün

word kelime
work (noun) iş
  (verb) çalışmak
worry beads tespih
worse daha kötü
worst en kötü
wrapping paper ambalaj kağıdı
wrist bilek
write yazmak
writing paper yazı kağıdı
wrong yanlış

year yıl
yellow sarı
yes evet
yesterday dün
yet henüz
  not yet henüz değil
yoghurt yoğurt
you (sing. polite and plural) siz
  (sing. familiar) sen
your: your book (polite) sizin kitabınız
  (familiar) senin kitabın
yours: is it yours? (polite) sizin mi?
  (familiar) senin mi?
youth hostel gençlik yurdu

zip fermuar
zoo hayvanat bahçesi